TIM
BURTON

For my mum, who'd have got a kick out of this

First published in Great Britain in 2025 by Greenfinch
An imprint of Quercus
Part of John Murray Group

A CIP catalogue record for this book is available from the British Library

ISBN 978-1-52944-716-3
EBOOK ISBN 978-1-52944-717-0

10 9 8 7 6 5 4 3 2 1

Cover design by Luke Bird
Interior design by Ginny Zeal
Printed and bound in Dubai by Oriental Press

Papers used by Quercus are from well-managed forests and other responsible sources.

Quercus
Carmelite House
50 Victoria Embankment
London EC4Y 0DZ

John Murray Group
Part of Hodder & Stoughton Limited
An Hachette UK company

The authorised representative in the EEA is Hachette Ireland,
8 Castlecourt Centre, Dublin 15, D15 XTP3, Ireland (email: info@hbgi.ie)

TIM BURTON

THE COMPLETE UNOFFICIAL GUIDE

OLLY RICHARDS

greenfinch

CONTENTS

'If I could prescribe a single rule for looking at a work of art it would be to enjoy it. If we're honest with ourselves, we have to admit we enjoy our tears just as much as we enjoy our laughter. The only moments of life that are a bore are when we don't care one way or another.'

VINCENT PRICE,
FROM *I LIKE WHAT I KNOW: A VISUAL AUTOBIOGRAPHY*

ABOVE: Michael Keaton as the title character in *Beetlejuice, Beetlejuice*, a role he reprised 36 years after the original.

INTRODUCTION

Tim Burton is the first movie director I was ever aware of. His were not the first films I *saw*, but in my earliest years it didn't really occur to me that there was anyone behind the camera actually making films. My still-forming brain assumed that Tom Hanks, Eddie Murphy or the cast of *The Goonies* just wandered onto screen and made up a story. Then *Batman* came out.

I was nine years old when the 1989 *Batman* was released. It seemed omnipresent. There were posters everywhere. Toy shops were full of merchandise. And this Tim Burton person was always popping up on TV, or being talked about as a wunderkind who had redefined the blockbuster. In interviews, he looked just like some regular guy, reluctant to make eye contact, seemingly allergic to the ends of sentences. Discovering not only that *people* make movies, but people like this man made movies, opened up my tiny mind. As a fairly nerdy kid, it was a big deal to see a grown-up nerd doing cool things. It was a couple more years before I was allowed to actually watch *Batman*, but I became devoted to Burton for years thereafter.

It was initially quite a shallow devotion, largely based on aesthetics. Particularly in those early days, Burton was a visual master. He's one of the few directors whose films you can identify within a few frames. His Brothers Grimm meets German expressionism meets pastel suburbia style is unlike anything else. His films don't all look the same – *Batman Returns* isn't like *Ed Wood* isn't like *Big Fish* isn't like *Beetlejuice* – yet there's a graphic quality that pulls them all together.

The strength of his visuals has seen Burton repeatedly dismissed as just a purveyor of pretty pictures and popcorn movies, not a *serious* filmmaker. Yet the more of his films that you watch, the more you see the emotional intelligence and curiosity he has. Almost all of his movies work on a similar theme – that of outsiders – and he finds endless ways to explore that. Boiled down to their essence, *Batman* and *Ed Wood* are about the same thing: a person who doesn't fit in and doesn't fully understand why. But they couldn't be more different as films. Burton's entire career could be read as learning to love being the odd one out.

Even the biggest fan would surely admit there have been bad times. *Mars Attacks!* was Burton's first major misfire, a film with a confusing lack of heart, that feels like a joke the audience isn't in

BELOW: Willy Wonka's world, in Burton's 2005 adaptation of Roald Dahl's *Charlie and the Chocolate Factory*.

on. *Planet of the Apes* was such a disaster that Burton rarely talks about it still, and the iffy films became more frequent in the 2010s. Yet, every time Burton is written off, he comes back with something that reminds you how spellbinding he can be. After *Mars Attacks!* came the Hammer Horror-ish fun of *Sleepy Hollow.* After *Planet of the Apes,* we get the emotional outpouring of *Big Fish.* Burton will always come up with a way to surprise you.

The first time I met Tim Burton was on the set of *Charlie and the Chocolate Factory.* This was in 2004, when more and more movies were being shot against green screen and a lot of Hollywood films were developing a dreary, identikit digital sheen. *Charlie* had full practical sets, with a gushing chocolate waterfall, towering factory, and Charlie Bucket's rickety house at full scale. Burton insisted on it. That's part of his beauty. He has huge respect for craft and understands the indefinable difference it makes to an audience to know that everything they're watching was there. In the times I have met him since, I think the most energetic I've ever seen him was on the set of the stop-motion animated *Frankenweenie.* Stop-motion exemplifies Burton's love of doing things for real. Moving tiny models a fraction of a centimetre, over and over, to make a second of cinema is an absurdly labour-intensive way to make a movie, but when you see the result, it's magic. You can't see the fingerprints, but you can sense them.

While this isn't a Burton biography, the story of Burton's films also has to be, to some degree, the story of the man. Most of his films are personal, because he's the eternal misfit. Pee-wee Herman, Edward Scissorhands, Jack Skellington, even Catwoman, are all Burton to an extent. Viewed as a whole, his films are the journey of a man finding himself, losing himself a couple of times, then rediscovering his early joy. Burton already has more than 20 directing projects to his name, but I believe his best may still be to come.

NO
ORDINARY
KID

As a child, Tim Burton spent a lot of time in the graveyard. Several of his relatives are buried in Valhalla Memorial Park, but that isn't why he went there. 'It was a good place to think', he figured. It was one of the only places in Burbank he actually liked. He could sit there for hours, drawing, making up stories, imagining a life more interesting than this.

Burbank is a peculiar Los Angeles suburb. It's just a few miles northeast of Hollywood, the world capital of movie-making, yet somehow feels a million miles from it, almost entirely untouched by its glamour. Burton was born here in 1958, growing up on one of many streets of boxy houses, full of typical American families, like Burton's. His dad worked for the city Parks and Recreation department and his mother owned a cat-themed gift shop. He didn't know where he fitted in to this wholesome picture. Burton, who didn't much like school and wasn't much good at it, spent a lot of his time retreating into movies. At the time, Burbank's big claim to fame was that it was home to the headquarters of Walt Disney, but that wasn't especially interesting to Burton. His cinematic passions lay in darker places.

'My first film school was the Cornell Theater', Burton once said of the cinema where he spent many childhood days, often settling in for 50-cent triple bills of cheesy monster pictures, such as *Monster Zero* (1965), *War of the Gargantuas* (1966) and *Kill All Monsters* (1968). Burton adored monster movies – his mother said he was never afraid of any horror – and devoured them in many forms. He loved the Universal monster films of the 1930s: *Dracula* (1931), *Frankenstein* (1931) and *The Mummy* (1932). He loved the more lurid creature features coming out of Japan, like *Godzilla* (1954), and everything produced by Britain's Hammer

RIGHT: *War of the Gargantuas*, one of many monster features that inspired the young Burton.

Burton on TV

After directing *Frankenweenie* in 1984, Burton was invited to direct an episode of Faerie Tale Theatre. The series, which dramatized popular kids' stories, was the brainchild of *Frankenweenie* star Shelley Duvall. Broadcast in 1986, Burton's take on *Aladdin* is cute, in a rather unpolished way, with a surprisingly good cast. James Earl Jones plays a menacing blue genie and Leonard Nimoy is an evil magician.

Also aired in 1986, *The Jar*, an episode of *Alfred Hitchcock Presents*, was about a container that holds something very bizarre. Largely set in an art gallery, it's extremely kitsch, with hints of the goth-pop-art styling that was all over *Beetlejuice*. It would be almost 40 years until he would direct TV again, with *Wednesday*.

Productions. He especially liked anything featuring the work of Ray Harryhausen, the stop-motion legend who created the skeleton sword fight in *Jason and the Argonauts* (1963) and the many-armed Kali in *The Golden Voyage of Sinbad* (1973).

Burton would spend hours drawing his own creatures, dreaming up adventures of his own. As a teenager, he began to experiment with directing, using a Super-8 camera to make rough stop-motion animation shorts, inspired by the likes of *When Dinosaurs Ruled the Earth* (1970) or H G Wells' *The Island of Doctor Moreau* (1896). He tried live action too, roping in school friends to flesh out his cast. Like pretty much any kid with a camera, his skill was rough, but his ideas were limitless. He wasn't making any of it to be seen by other people; it was just for him.

At school, it never occurred to him that he might eventually be able to make films for a living. He just wanted to create stuff. But once he graduated, with no idea what else he might be suited to, he wondered if his drawing might be his way into filmmaking. 'I couldn't imagine getting a real job', he said. With limited opportunities, he turned to a place that could not have suited him less.

Disney animation was at a difficult point in the mid-70s. Well past its golden days, the studio was releasing films like *The Aristocats* (1970) and *Robin Hood* (1973) – perfectly decent, but far below the quality of a decade earlier, and hits like *101 Dalmations* (1961) and *The Jungle Book* (1967). The problem was its key creative team had barely changed since the 1950s. They were very talented people, but from another era, and now very old. Disney needed new blood, so it set up a scholarship programme as a training ground for the next generation of animated filmmakers. That's how, in 1976, at the age of 18, Burton found himself at California Institute of the Arts, studying character animation.

From the start, it wasn't his natural environment. His classmates were people who would later become some of the defining animation directors of our time, such as John Musker (*Aladdin*; 1992), John Lasseter (*Toy Story*; 1995) and Brad Bird (*Ratatouille*; 2007), but Burton couldn't do what they did. His drawings were spiky and rough, nothing like the cute, smooth, Disney style. He *tried* to fit in. It was here, in 1979, that he made his first proper film, his graduation piece, *Stalk of the Celery Monster*. For a kid still only just into his 20s, it's remarkably good. A loose take on the story of Frankenstein, it features a seemingly crazed scientist operating on a terrified woman. Cackling as he advances on her with an enormous drill, the 'scientist' is revealed to be not a depraved madman, but merely a possibly depraved dentist. It's witty, expressively drawn, and although it has had the edges rounded off, you can see things that would become Burton hallmarks: angular limbs, wild hair, saucer eyes with pinprick pupils. It was nutty, but good enough that Disney offered Burton a job in its animation department. He didn't hugely *want* to become a Disney animator, but it was a job making films, and he definitely wanted that.

. . .Until he didn't. Burton's first assignment was doing background work for the 1981 film *The Fox and the Hound*, but all his foxes looked 'like roadkill'. 'I didn't flourish in that environment', he said. 'In some ways it was good for me, because they took me out of that and I was able, for a year or so, just to do conceptual work.' Unsure of what to do with his obvious, if not very Disney, talent, his bosses took him off *The Fox and the Hound,* set him up in his own office, and told him to draw

BELOW: An early sketch for *Vincent*, the stop-motion short film that kick-started Burton's career.

whatever he wanted. He invented some monsters for *The Black Cauldron* (1985), one of Disney's least fondly regarded films. They were never used. He started drawing a children's book, *Vincent*, about a young, lonely boy who dreams of being like the actor Vincent Price, living in a horror movie, not boring real life. Price was one of Burton's heroes. He'd always loved his movies, including *Masque of the Red Death* (1964) and *Theatre of Blood* (1973). He liked that Price always played tortured outcasts, because that's exactly how Burton felt.

He envisaged *Vincent* as a stop-motion film. Two Disney executives, Julie Hickson and Tom Wilhite, gave Burton $60,000 to develop it, considering it a worthwhile experiment into stop-motion animation. If it worked, maybe the studio would want to do something bigger in the future. So, recruiting fellow animator Rick Heinrichs, who would become a treasured collaborator through Burton's whole career, and a couple of others, he created a six-minute film. With the boldness of youth, Burton even approached the actual Vincent Price and asked him if he might narrate it. To his astonishment, Price said yes.

Vincent was a creative turning point for Burton. Instead of trying to bend himself to fit what was expected of him, he'd made something that was 100 per cent true to himself, and a lot of people liked it. *Vincent* played at a few short film festivals and won acclaim. Unsurprisingly, Disney considered it too dark to release. The studio did, however, believe in Burton's talent enough to offer him more opportunities to express it.

His next project was a version of *Hansel and Gretel*, his first attempt at long-form live action. Made in 1983 for the newly launched Disney Channel, it's a nightmarish, quite awkwardly acted film, but visually it's a riot. Burton's personality is all over it, from the witch's candy-cane nose, to a twisted gingerbread house, to his trademark skeletal trees. It was sufficiently well received for Disney to entrust Burton with $1 million to make a film that would set his career rocketing.

When Burton was small, his family had two dogs: Frosty and Pepe. Frosty was your regular happy, yappy canine, but Pepe, Burton's favourite, always had the sword of Damocles hanging over his fluffy little head. Born with distemper, Pepe wasn't expected to live long. Yet somehow, miraculously, he just kept going, making it to a perfectly regular dog age. 'It just had a good spirit, that dog', said Burton. That acute awareness of a pet's mortality, and the constant fear it may die any minute, morphed into the plot of his short film *Frankenweenie*.

Another spin on the story of Frankenstein, it follows young Victor Frankenstein (Barret Oliver), an amateur scientist and filmmaker. Victor is devoted to his dog, Sparky, his constant companion and star of many of his homemade pictures. When Sparky is run over and killed, Victor's devastated, but he manages to figure out the science that will bring Sparky back to life. The resurrected Sparky is still the same loyal pet to Victor, despite his many stitches and neck bolts, but he terrifies the neighbours so much that, in an echo of the climax of James Whale's 1931 *Frankenstein*, they chase him with pitchforks to a showdown at a windmill; although this windmill is in the local mini golf course.

As well as being Burton's most ambitious production so far, *Frankenweenie* was also his first time directing well-known actors. Shelley Duvall, best remembered for the 1980 movie *The Shining*, played Victor's mother. Daniel Stern, who would later secure his place in film history as Marv in *Home Alone* (1990) took on Victor's father. It's a tremendously imaginative, blackly comic film, but it marked the end of Burton's days at Disney.

The studio had considered playing it in front of a re-release of *Pinocchio*, but got cold feet, reasoning that dog death would be just too upsetting for children (nevermind the many disturbing horrors in *Pinocchio*). After entrusting Burton with well over a million dollars on his multiple projects, they had, they thought, nothing releasable to show for it. Burton was invited to seek employment elsewhere.

No matter. *Frankenweenie* may not have been a hit with Disney, but it had won him some very influential fans. Though he didn't yet realize it, thanks to that unique little film, Burton's career as a film director was about to begin.

BELOW: Sparky the dog rescues Victor, played by Barret Oliver, in *Frankenweenie*.

'Let's turn on the juice and see what shakes loose'

THE BREAKOUT YEARS

PEE-WEE'S BIG ADVENTURE
1985

Typically, getting your debut movie off the ground requires many years of hard effort and countless knockbacks. For Tim Burton, however, landing his first gig as a feature director was, he says, 'Easier than getting my restaurant job at Sir George's Smorgasbord.' If only all his future projects had been as straightforward as this.

There are differing accounts of just how *Pee-wee's Big Adventure* came to Burton. In Burton's telling, he was brought on by Bonni Lee, an executive at Warner Bros, who'd spotted something in him after watching *Frankenweenie*. According to Paul Reubens, the film's star, who died in 2023, it was he who suggested Burton. Whoever it was that had the idea, it was *exactly* the right choice.

An icon in the United States, Pee-wee Herman is less well known beyond its borders, and it's difficult to describe him to anyone who has never watched him. Created by Reubens in the late 1970s, when he was part of improvisation troupe The Groundlings, Pee-wee was originally styled as a useless stand-up comic, with an awkward manner, foghorn laugh and weird outfit of too-small grey suit and prissy red bow tie. Over time, the character evolved into part satire of, part tribute to American children's entertainers of the 1950s; the sort who affected an eternal-child energy and were usually friends with puppets. He was at once wholesome and optimistic, and ever so slightly sinister.

In 1981, HBO aired *The Pee-wee Herman Show*, a staged special featuring a fairly adults-only version of the character (at one point Pee-wee 'hypnotizes' a woman and instructs her to strip). It was a cult hit and Reubens toured the character in live shows across the United States. On the back of its success, Warner Bros commissioned Reubens to write a low-budget film script, which he did, along with Phil Hartman and Michael Varhol. But, according to Reubens, Warner Bros' choice of director didn't *get* Pee-wee.

'I was basically looking for a director other than the one the studio wanted to use', said Reubens. At a party, he said, he was talking to a friend, jobbing actor and writer Maryedith Burrell, about his difficulty finding a director who understood what he was trying to do. Burrell had recently seen *Frankenweenie* and insisted Reubens watch it, then meet Tim Burton. Within the first minute of watching *Frankenweenie,* Reubens knew Burton was the guy. 'He had a really strong sense of style and he was somebody really informed by art direction. Those were two things I was looking for', said Reubens. They met and got on immediately, bonding over the same film and art references. Burton had the job without so much as pitching. He was only 26 at the time.

Warner Bros' struggle to find a director for *Pee-wee's Big Adventure* is understandable. It's a very odd script, with the merest wisp of a

RIGHT: Paul Reubens as Pee-wee, a character he invented in the 1970s and continued to play for more than 40 years.

plot. Pee-wee, who lives alone in a cartoonish house full of elaborate gadgets, giant toys and a tiny dog, is very much in love with his red bicycle. So much so, that he keeps it locked in a secret vault. One day, while Pee-wee is buying magic tricks, his bike is stolen. Devastated, he embarks on a quest to get it back. That's basically the whole plot. For most directors, it isn't a lot to work with. For Burton, it was like a huge caffeine jolt to his imagination.

'I believed Pee-wee,' said Burton. 'So, I thought, let's just go through the movie and believe him, whatever he does.' Burton treats Pee-wee's ridiculousness seriously. There's no attempt to explain why he is the way he is, nor why everybody he encounters accepts this honking little oddball's behaviour as completely reasonable. Under Burton's direction, the misfit sets the tone. It's tempting to read it as Burton reframing reality as he would like it

The Music Man

On *Pee-wee,* Burton formed one of his most lasting working relationships. When looking for someone to score the film, both he and Paul Reubens thought of Danny Elfman. Reubens had enjoyed *Forbidden Zone* (1980) a film by Elfman's brother, Richard, for which Elfman had written some music. That was his only experience of scoring. Burton was a fan of Oingo Boingo, the punk band Elfman fronted. They thought Elfman might fit Pee-wee's surreal outlook.

When Burton asked to meet, Elfman just assumed Burton wanted to use one of his songs. Elfman asked, '"Why me?" And he said, "I think you could do a score". It was pretty weird, because I really hadn't thought about composing.'

The partnership was so successful that Elfman has gone on to score all but two of Burton's films, missing only *Ed Wood* and, because it already had a score, the musical *Sweeney Todd.* His other claim to fame is composing the theme to *The Simpsons.*

to be, where nobody asks you why you are behaving like that and why you can't just be *normal*.

Pee-wee is more a parade of sketches, all tumbling into each other, than a traditionally structured film. They don't all work, but there's so much invention on show. The opening sequence alone is a triumph of creativity. It's just Pee-wee waking up and making breakfast, but that involves a giant Heath Robinson-type contraption, in which orange juice is squeezed by a dinosaur skeleton and pancakes are flipped by a bust of Abraham Lincoln. It's wonderful.

It was, in a way, a kind of mini film school for Burton. 'I got to play in so many funny little genres that it felt quite easy', he said. There was comedy, of course. He tried a bit of horror, with a clown-based nightmare sequence. There's action, in the film's climactic chase, which sees Pee-wee riding through a film studio, careening through sets for a Christmas movie, a 60s-style beach movie and a Twisted Sister music video shoot. There's a Buster Keatonesque race to rescue animals from a burning pet shop. And, in the film's best sequence, in which Pee-wee hitches a ride with trucker Large Marge, Burton got the opportunity to use his beloved stop-motion animation. Marge, it turns out, is a ghost and briefly transforms into a monster.

Watching *Pee-wee*, you can see the beginnings of Burton's signature style. There's none of the polish that would come later – visually, its grubby gaudiness almost resembles the work of John Waters, the king of trash cinema (*Pink Flamingos*, 1972, *Hairspray*, 1988) – but there are signs of what he would become. The dream sequence features the black-and-white motif and wonky perspective that became trademarks, and there's a handmade quality to all of it. That was probably a necessity of budget here, yet it's something Burton has maintained. He likes his work to be imperfect.

More than anything, you can see the birth of a theme that has continued through most of Burton's films: people existing in eternal adolescence, living a little bit outside of society. Pee-wee is an eccentric who has no intention of changing himself. At one point, he tells Dottie (E G Daily), a bike shop employee who mystifyingly has the hots for him, 'I'm a loner, Dottie. A rebel'. Burton has a love of loners who don't fit in – Edward Scissorhands, Batman, Jack Skellington – and Pee-wee was his first.

Pee-wee's Big Adventure has achieved cult status over time, but reviews on release were, at best, mixed. While there were positives – the *Los Angeles Times* called it 'a comic odyssey' – the more common response was bemusement. Vincent Canby of *The New York Times* called it 'the most barren comedy I've seen in years, maybe ever'. Paul Attanasio of *The Washington Post* dismissed it as 'a collection of found objects from the garbage heap of low culture'. Audiences felt differently. On a reported budget of $7 million, *Pee-wee's Big Adventure* made $40 million at the box office. Burton was no critical darling, but he had a hit.

And *that*'s what gets you your next job.

Later in his career, Burton would say that getting poor reviews so early on was the best lesson he could have been given. 'It taught me the weirdness of the whole thing', he said. 'It balanced me out. I didn't get egotistical about it.' He thought the alternative – being immediately lauded and having to live up to that pressure – would be a far worse scenario. And besides, it worked out for everyone. With the birth of his kids' TV show, *Pee-wee's Playhouse,* the following year, Pee-wee Herman grew into a US national treasure. And Burton was now a bankable filmmaker, so his next step was to do what any right-thinking filmmaker would do: make the craziest film imaginable.

ABOVE: Pee-wee (Paul Reubens) on his beloved red bicycle, a Schwinn DX Cruiser.

BEETLEJUICE
1988

Had things gone a little differently, this chapter would be all about Tim Burton's talking horse movie.

After declining a *Pee-wee* sequel, Burton wasn't short on offers. Unfortunately, they were mostly from producers who wanted him to do what he had done on *Pee-wee*: turn an unpromising script into box-office gold. That was exemplified by *Hot to Trot*, a screenplay about a man who shares a flat with a talking horse. Burton immediately turned it down (it would go on to be directed by Michael Dinner, with John Candy voicing the

ABOVE: Alec Baldwin as Adam. He later recalled thinking the film, which he didn't understand, might end his career.

horse; it wasn't a success). The ease with which he had landed his first directing gig was clearly not to be repeated.

The three years between his first and second films weren't spent twiddling his thumbs. Burton had been hired by Warner Bros to work on ideas for a potential *Batman* movie, but the studio was nowhere near ready to greenlight it. And he was noodling away on an idea about Jack Skellington, a character he'd been drawing since childhood. Those were both on the back burner, but his front burner was empty. Then someone gave him the most bizarre script in Hollywood at the time, and it would become his defining movie.

The screenplay for *Beetlejuice* had existed for a while before it fell into Burton's hands. Michael McDowell was a successful and very prolific horror novelist and occasional TV writer (*Amazing Stories,*

ABOVE: Geena Davis as Barbara, the recently deceased woman who unwittingly summons Betelgeuse.

Alfred Hitchcock Presents) who had designs on cinema. He was, by his own admission, a commercial writer and was looking to write a *hit* not *art*. *Poltergeist*, Tobe Hooper's horror movie, had been a success in 1982, and McDowell thought something ghostly might be his way in.

McDowell and his partner had been having some problems with their neighbours, which led him to a very clever idea: What if, instead of people being terrified by the ghosts in their house, the ghosts were annoyed by humans invading their home? He expanded the concept into a script with Larry Wilson, a story analyst – that is, somebody who finds good screenplays for studios. For two people whose careers up to this point had been all about generating commercial ideas, their collaboration led to something decidedly anti-mainstream.

If you think the final *Beetlejuice* script is crackers, it's positively tame compared to early versions. At its heart were always the Maitlands, Barbara and Adam, who live in their dream home in a bucolic little town and have a very happy life. That is, until they die in a freak car accident. In initial drafts, the Maitlands suffer horrible deaths. When they're run off a bridge by a van full of hunters, Barbara's arm is gruesomely crushed and they drown slowly, in close-up, as their car is buffeted along a raging river.

They find no peace in death. Their home, which their spirits can't leave, is bought by the horrible Deetzes, a pair of brittle New Yorkers, Charles and Delia, who move in with awkward nine-year-old Cathy and Lydia, a 16-year-old daughter from Charles's first marriage. Lydia is a hipster going through a goth phase. In an effort to be rid of the Deetzes, the Maitlands summon Betelgeuse (nobody seems to know why the spelling in the film doesn't match the title). In this version he's a small and wiry, snake-eyed demon, bent on killing the Deetzes and making Lydia his lover (reminder that she's 16). It's still a comedy, but much, much darker.

RIGHT: Lydia (Winona Ryder) celebrates a house free of Betelgeuse. She was just 15 when she played the role.

CHAPTER TWO

'This piece of crap is going to sink you', was the reaction when Wilson first showed the script to a studio. Fortunately, someone else had a more positive reaction. Wilson taught a story analysis class at UCLA. His smartest pupil, Marjorie Lewis, had a junior position at The Geffen Company, a small production company run by David Geffen that had had some success with *Risky Business* (1983) and *Little Shop of Horrors* (1986). A dejected Lewis asked her if she liked the script at all: 'Like it? I'm going to get the Geffen Company to buy it.'

When the script came to Burton (The Geffen Company was owned by Warner Bros, which produced *Pee-wee's Big Adventure*), he immediately loved it. 'It was amazing because it was the exact opposite of everything else I'd gotten', Burton said at the time. 'Most of these scripts were like A to B to C, all tied up in a neat little package. Then I get this script that makes no sense!' Burton wanted to make it, but as soon as he signed on, the studio started looking at the script more closely. They did *not* want to make this. After an exhausting parade of meetings in which executives tried to water the film down and Burton tried to resist them, his agents put him in a room with another of their clients, writer Warren Skaaren. Skaaren was considered a whizz at knocking rough scripts into shape. He'd done an uncredited polish on *Top Gun* (1986) and was working on punching up *Beverly Hills Cop 2* (1987).

Skaaren managed to keep the script's gonzo edge while making it more palatable to the studio. The Maitlands' deaths would be off-screen, which had the bonus of being much cheaper. Cathy and Lydia were combined into a smart, ghost-sensitive teen. And Betelgeuse, while still a maniac, was no longer homicidal and was marginally less sexually troubling. The final script is credited to McDowell and Skaaren, with story by McDowell and Wilson.

ABOVE: Delia (Catherine O'Hara) in the 'Day-O' scene. Harry Belafonte's music was chosen mostly because it was cheap.

Script approved, Burton started the search for his title character. While he's always been something of a genius when it comes to casting, he was maybe off his game when it came to Betelgeuse. He wanted Sammy Davis Jr. Geffen flatly refused, but he had a suggestion of his own.

In the mid-80s, Michael Keaton's star was looking a bit scuffed. His biggest hit up to this point was 1983's *Mr. Mom*, an amiable comedy that asks what might happen if a man became a stay-at-home parent (ah, the 80s). And even that success was well in the past. He was on a dud streak. He needed a hit, and he didn't think *Beetlejuice* was it. On Geffen's suggestion, he met Burton, then turned the role down.

'I had no idea what he was talking about when he was pitching me *Beetlejuice*', Keaton remembered. Burton, however, thought Keaton had something worth pursuing. He asked him to reconsider

ABOVE: The quaint Winter River, Connecticut, setting for the film was actually the Vermont town of East Corinth.

and to tell him what he would do with the character. Keaton came back with an explosion of thoughts. The thing he seized on was the idea that 'the character creates his own reality'. Other people's behaviour is almost invisible to Betelgeuse. As far as he's concerned, everyone loves everything about him. He envisioned him looking completely disgusting, to make the self-esteem even more incongruous. Keaton began creating Betelgeuse from 'the outside in'. The wild hair was his idea. The crusty skin was him. As was the voice. He was onboard.

Most of the rest of the cast fell into place reasonably easily. Geena Davis loved the script and signed on for Barbara. Alec Baldwin didn't really get the script, and said as much when the film was released, but took the role of Adam. Jeffrey Jones and Catherine O'Hara would be Charles and Delia Deetz. O'Hara, then little known, was a last-minute addition when Angelica Huston had to drop out. And in the role of Lydia was another of Burton's brilliant discoveries.

Winona Ryder was only 15 when she auditioned for *Beetlejuice*, with just two films to her name, *Lucas* (1986) and *Square Dance* (1987). As she sat in an office on the Warner Bros lot, nervously waiting to meet her potential director, a gawky young man came in and began chatting to her. It was a welcome distraction – they found a mutual affection for the art of Edward Gorey – and he helped her pass the time for about 45 minutes. Eventually, she had to ask, 'Where's this Tim Burton guy?'. The man replied, 'That's me'. She had no idea this was Burton and she had been auditioning for close to an hour: 'I thought he was from the art department.'

Burton and Ryder were kindred misfits. Both dressed head to toe in black and hiding shyly behind their hair, they felt like aliens in the film world. And that was exactly what Burton wanted for Lydia: someone with the inner steel to try to make it in movies/take on an underworld monster, but also an innate vulnerability. Burton had seen a lot of young, very talented actors for Lydia – Brooke Shields, Sarah Jessica Parker, Jennifer Connelly – but Ryder had the exact something he needed. Once Ryder had realized her mistake in that meeting, she asked Burton, 'Do you want me to read?'. He said, 'No, I want you to do it.'

Shooting took place early in 1987, on Warner Bros sound stages and on location in the picturesque Vermont town of East Corinth. It was, by all accounts, a joy. Burton, with more than double the budget he'd had on *Pee-wee*, was tremendously enjoying figuring things out with creative people. He hired contributors who would become part of his team, on and off, for decades, like production designer Bo Welch and visual effects consultant (later production designer) Rick Heinrichs. 'The things that interest me the most are the things that potentially won't work', he said, and what he loved here was finding ways to make things work. A lot of the film's best moments were figured out while shooting. Nowhere is this better illustrated than in the dinner table scene where the Deetzes and their guests are possessed and begin involuntarily dancing to Harry Belafonte's song 'Banana Boat (Day-O)'.

While rehearsing, Burton couldn't work out how to shoot the climactic moment, when the dishes of big pink prawns turn into hands and grab the guests' faces. He had people under the table playing the prawn hands, but unable to see where they were reaching, they kept punching the actors in the face. It was Glenn Shadix (playing the horrible Otho), who suggested they shoot that

sequence in reverse, so the actors began with their faces in the bowl, then get pushed backwards. Then Burton could simply play it backwards. It worked perfectly.

Burton was attracted to *Beetlejuice* because it made 'no sense', and if the finished film is a lot more coherent than that early draft, it's still a movie full of plot holes you could ride a sandworm through – one of those being, 'What's the deal with the sandworms?' – but that's a large part of why it's such a hoot. It's cheerful anarchy, a surrealist joy, centred on a lunatic turn from Keaton. *Beetlejuice* showed Burton wasn't just a brilliant visual technician but an actors' director. A performance like Keaton's, which Keaton called 'rave

acting', is only possible with a director who lets an actor go wild, but knows where the limit is. There's nothing self-indulgent. It's all for the audience.

Just as happened with *Pee-wee*, reviews for *Beetlejuice* were mixed. Roger Ebert, one of America's biggest critics, hated it. Pauline Kael, arguably the most important critic in history, enjoyed it, saying Burton 'has a kid's delight in the homegrown surreal' and calling the whole film 'blossoming chaos', which is about right. *Beetlejuice* is Burton growing into himself, discovering himself as a filmmaker. If the training wheels were still on for *Pee-wee*, they had now flown off. He was about to become the biggest young director in Hollywood.

LEFT: Betelgeuse (Michael Keaton) makes his point.

'Where does he get those wonderful toys?'

THE
GAME
CHANGER

BATMAN
1989

Back in the mid-1980s, superhero movies had little of the prestige they have now. The first two *Superman* movies were huge hits, in 1978 and 1980, but otherwise the genre was littered with flops. Warner Bros had been kicking around a potential Batman movie since 1980, commissioning ten scripts by ten different writers, yet none of them were quite right.

Multiple directors had come and gone, including Joe Dante (*Gremlins*; 1984) and Ivan Reitman (*Ghostbusters*; 1984). One script, by Tom Mankiewicz, came very close to being made, because it was essentially *Superman* with a different outfit, aping the same bright tone and hitting very similar story beats. But even that couldn't make it across the line. By the middle of the decade, the studio had lost enthusiasm and let *Batman* fall into the shadows. Then two rookies emerged to save it.

In 1986, Sam Hamm was nobody's idea of a star writer. He had one credit, a small 1983 eco-drama called *Never Cry Wolf*, and a bunch of unproduced scripts. Nevertheless, Warner Bros put him under contract, working on various potential movies. One day, while on a wander round the studio, Hamm found a copy of Mankiewicz's *Batman* script. He knew the studio was having problems with it and he couldn't understand why. 'It didn't seem to me that *Batman* would be all that hard to do', said Hamm. He thought Mankiewicz had it wrong, telling the story of how Bruce Wayne became Batman, which he considered the least interesting aspect of the character's story. 'It's essentially a regular guy dressed up in a suit', he said. He thought there was a better way to approach it.

With nothing to lose, he contacted a friend, Bonni Lee, the executive who'd championed Tim Burton on *Pee-wee,* and asked if he could try writing *Batman*. He was unaware that Warner Bros had recently acquired Burton as a potential new director. A meeting was arranged.

Burton and Hamm came from different perspectives, but matching visions. Burton had never really read the comics but liked the dual nature of Bruce Wayne's personality and his outsider status. Hamm grew up reading the comics, but didn't want to do the vintage 'BLAM! KAPOW!' version with comedy gadgets and underpants over tights. 'The first thing we talked about was that

ABOVE: Michael Keaton as Bruce Wayne. Keaton's casting was met with significant backlash from fans.

we wanted to do it straight and scary and psychological', said Hamm of his meeting with Burton. Around this time, the Batman comics were undergoing a grittier, more serious renaissance with Frank Miller's 1986 *The Dark Knight Returns* and Alan Moore's 1988 *The Killing Joke*. This was more the tone the pair wanted.

Hamm wrote a script that began with Bruce Wayne already established as Batman. A photojournalist, Vicki Vale, is fascinated by the antihero's repeat appearances and wants to find out who's behind the mask. Little does she know the man she's dating, Bruce Wayne, is Batman's alter-ego. When not romancing, Batman is trying to thwart a deadly plot by laughing killer, Joker.

Warner Bros liked Hamm's script, but the film didn't get the official go ahead until the weekend *Beetlejuice* opened. When that took $8 million in three days, on a $15 million budget, Burton was officially a bankable director. *Batman* was on.

It was at this point the negative press started. 'They thought I was going to do, like, Adam West', Burton said years later. The comedy and colour of *Pee-wee* and *Beetlejuice* led people to assume his *Batman* would be similar to the 1960s *Batman* TV show, but Burton had not yet shown everything in his playbook. His take on Batman would bring in influences from all those horror movies he loved, with their mad scientists, split personalities and expressionist aesthetic.

Rather than tell the story of a boy becoming Batman, Burton and Hamm's script peels away Batman's layers to understand the man beneath the cowl. Burton doesn't care about people *becoming* freaks. He's interested in how freaks deal with the world. His Batman had to be an actor who could play the complexity, not an action lunk who could fill a supersuit. It was producer Jon Peters who suggested Michael Keaton.

Burton gave Keaton the script and asked him to just think about it. As he had with *Beetlejuice*, Keaton came back with a million ideas. They both saw Batman not as a beefy hero but a depressed guy working out his issues in a really unhealthy way. 'An odd dude', said Keaton. While they were not enthusiastic, Warner Bros agreed to the casting. Fans were apoplectic.

'*Batman* Fans Fear The Joke's On Them', ran the headline of a scathing *Wall Street Journal* article, indicative of the general media mood, which called Keaton an 'average Joe' and suggested Clint

LEFT: Kim Basinger as Vicki Vale. Sean Young was originally cast in the role but had to drop out following a pre-production injury.

Near Misses

Burton has a long filmography, but it might have been even longer. There have been many abandoned projects over the years. Early in his career, he wanted to make a musical version of the horror movie *House of Wax* (1953), with Michael Jackson in the lead. Jackson was keen, Burton said, but studios turned it down.

In the early 1990s, Burton worked for almost two years developing *Mary Reilly*, about a maid working in the home of part-time monster Dr Jekyll. He eventually departed in 1993 and Stephen Frears took over. The resulting film was a notorious flop. Another deftly dodged turkey was *Cabin Boy*, a 1994 comedy about a stuck-up young man who accidentally winds up on a fantastical shipping voyage. He opted out of directing, with Adam Resnick stepping in, but remained as producer. The film was a critical and commercial disaster.

In the mid-2000s, Burton spent several years attached to an adaptation of *Ripley's Believe It or Not*, with Jim Carrey playing the lead. Shooting was bumped several times and the studio, Paramount, worried that the potential budget was spiralling out of control. Burton moved on in 2008 and the film never made it in front of cameras.

Other films he almost made include *Maleficent*, *The Hunchback of Notre Dame* with Josh Brolin, and *Pinocchio*, with Robert Downey Jr.

Eastwood or Sylvester Stallone would be a more appropriate Bruce Wayne. Burton firmly disagreed. 'It would have been very easy to go for a square-jawed hulk, but if some guy is 6 foot 5 with gigantic muscles, and incredibly handsome, why does he need to put on an armoured Batsuit?' he wondered. 'Why wouldn't he just put on a ski mask and beat the daylights out of bad guys?' The same article was only moderately more positive about the studio's choice for Joker, Jack Nicholson, fearing Nicholson was going to be too silly.

If only they'd known what Burton was planning, which was very far from Adam West. 'It's about depression', said the filmmaker.

'It's about duality, it's about flip sides, it's about a person who's completely fucked and doesn't know what he's doing'. Bruce Wayne is a guy who doesn't know who he is and thinks becoming someone else might help. By contrast, his enemy is a guy overburdened with self-esteem.

When we're first introduced to Jack Napier (Jack Nicholson), a hoodlum who works for a big mob boss (Jack Palance), he's preening in a mirror. Napier loves who he is and loves his life of crime. When he's mutilated in a toxic waste accident, becoming Joker, he doesn't fret over his own hideous transformation, but plots to make everyone look like him by poisoning them all with a chemical called Smylex, which mutates people's faces into leering grins and reduces them to fatal giggles. As Sam Hamm put it, his rationale is, 'If I can't wear slippers, I'm going to carpet the world. If this is what I'm going to look like, it's what everybody's going to look like.'

Audiences knew none of that yet and they gave Burton no benefit of the doubt. He was off to a difficult start.

Batman was meant to be an inexpensive project, originally budgeted at around $30 million, but costs ballooned from the start. Burton envisaged a Gotham that looked like a 1940s architect's idea of the 1980s, with a kind of art deco modernism. Terry Gilliam's 1985 masterpiece *Brazil*, with its beautiful, imposing buildings, was a key touchstone (Burton would hire that film's cinematographer, Roger Pratt). Almost the entirety of the United Kingdom's 95-acre (38-hectare) Pinewood Studios was taken over with Gotham sets.

The giant production necessitated 300 crew, many of whom were bemused by the shy young man leading them. Burton didn't have time to feel nervous. There was far too much to do. *Batman* wasn't an easy shoot. Despite a good reaction to Hamm's script,

Warner Bros asked for significant rewrites, which Hamm couldn't complete due to a strike by the Writers Guild of America. Revisions were instead completed by Warren Skaaren, who had got *Beetlejuice* into shootable shape, and an uncredited Charles McKeown (*The Adventures of Baron Munchausen*). Pages were being rewritten during production, so that Burton would sometimes be shooting the beginning of a scene with no idea how it was going to end.

Warner Bros was unhappy with the film's original finale. After a spectacular parade set piece, in which Joker tries to destroy Gotham with giant balloons filled with Smylex, only for Batman to whisk them away in his Batwing plane, they felt it lost momentum. The planned ending of the film took place at the top of Gotham Cathedral, where Batman and Joker have a showdown. Warner Bros wanted to add Vale (Kim Basinger) to the mix and make it all more dramatic. It was rewritten on the fly, leading to one memorable conversation where Nicholson asked why he and Vale were walking up the cathedral's hundreds of steps. Burton was unable to offer a response beyond, 'We'll talk about it when you get up to the top'. As intense as the shoot was, Keaton remembers a director who excelled under pressure. 'Tim seems to be, to me, someone who actually thrives on a lot of stuff going on at one time', he said.

Part of the tension around the shoot was due to the ongoing negative headlines about the production. In an effort to turn public opinion around, the studio rushed out a trailer for Christmas, six months ahead of release. A very scrappy affair, clearly edited from what was available halfway through the shoot, it fulfilled its purpose. It showed the film's stylish, brooding tone and hints of Keaton's serious performance. It was enough to quiet the moaning about both the actor and his look (fans had been up in arms about the Batman muscle suit, developed by people who specialized in fetish-wear). The hype for *Batman* had begun.

When *Batman* was released in the summer of 1989, audience response was ecstatic. It made $40.49 million in its opening weekend, a record at the time. Critics were positive, if not effusive. Of his own film, Burton later said, 'There's parts I liked, but it was a little boring at times', which is needlessly harsh on himself. It isn't perfect, but the vast majority of it is good.

It's a much more disciplined film than *Pee-wee* or *Beetlejuice*. Every frame is precisely composed and Burton has developed a far firmer grip on plot. He balances comedy and danger well, setting the tone brilliantly from the off. It starts with a great bait-

BELOW: The Batmobile, designed by Julian Caldow and Anton Furst.

ABOVE: Joker's alter ego Jack Napier (Jack Nicholson) tries to disguise his post-accident deformity.

and-switch. A stressed mother and father and their pre-teen son are trying unsuccessfully to hail a cab in scuzzy Gotham City. Bearings lost, they find themselves in a dark alley, where they are jumped by armed robbers. It's surely setting up the story of how Bruce Wayne becomes Batman, but then it cuts to a shadowy figure watching from far above, and Batman descends to punch out some bad guys. This is not, it tells the audience, an origin story.

Keaton proves inspired casting. One major criticism of the film was that it's more a Bruce Wayne movie than a Batman one, and Keaton's Wayne is much more interesting out of the suit, charismatic yet faintly awkward. In his first proper scene with Vicki Vale, he makes clumsy small talk and acts like a wallflower at his own party. He isn't, it seems, a man who relishes being a 'billionaire playboy'. Hamm says Wayne was much darker in his original drafts, but the balance of charmer and weirdo works. Wayne seems just unhinged enough to dress up and fly around the city, yet kind-hearted enough to always be on the side of good. And Keaton's underplaying balances the dialled-to-11 work of Nicholson, who chews an appropriate amount of scenery – that is, all of it.

There are parts that don't work. Vicki Vale is underwritten, mostly falling into the typical screaming damsel in distress role. And Nicholson had a point about the messy ending. Why – and more importantly how – *does* Joker walk up all those steps?

It isn't being entirely hyperbolic to call *Batman* one of the most influential films of the 20th century. It changed movie marketing, establishing the opening-weekend box office as a huge marker of a film's success, and turned studios on to the importance of 'teasing' movies months before release. More significantly, it set a blueprint for superhero movies that has been followed ever since. Every comic book movie started talking up its *darkness*. Offbeat casting became a badge of honour – think Heath Ledger as Joker or Tobey Maguire as Spider-Man. Silly tights gave way to sculpted 'armour'. And villains became the big selling point of any major superhero franchise. It wasn't about what the hero would do, but who they would fight. All this was established by Burton. If not for *Batman,* the current superhero landscape might look very different.

'I'm not finished'

THIS ONE'S FOR ME

EDWARD SCISSORHANDS
1990

'I felt very tortured as a teenager', said Tim Burton in 2012. 'That's where *Edward Scissorhands* came from. I was probably clinically depressed and didn't know it.' It's too straightforward to call *Edward Scissorhands* Burton's most personal film. It isn't about *him* or feelings unique to him. It's about the same themes he'd been exploring in all his films so far – feeling detached from the rest of society and finding ways to cope with that – but it explores them with a sensitivity he'd not expressed before. *Edward Scissorhands* is about someone who doesn't yet fully know how he fits into the world. If it isn't his most personal film – that's probably *Big Fish* – it's certainly his most vulnerable.

Having pulled off the biggest film hit of 1989, Burton should have been in a position to make whatever he wanted. Sadly, Hollywood has never worked like that. When he pitched *Edward Scissorhands* to Warner Bros it was a flat no. The studio wanted a *Batman* sequel, not. . .whatever this was. Burton took it down the street to 20th Century Fox, where he was assured of the one thing he absolutely required on this project: total creative control.

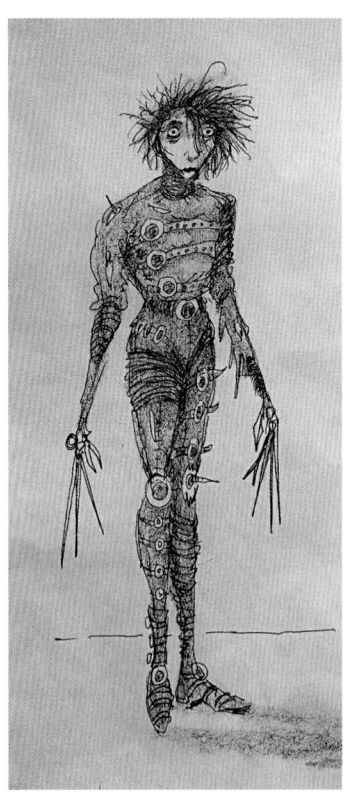

Edward Scissorhands had appeared in Burton's life without him really thinking about it. Some time in his teenage years – he forgets exactly when; he's not good with dates – Burton was sketching. He produced a picture of a skinny guy in a black suit, with wild hair and long, blade-like fingers. In retrospect, he could see that it represented everything he was feeling at the time: isolated, weird, unable to connect with people. 'I didn't grow up in a very tactile family', he said. 'If somebody hugged me, I would flinch, because I wasn't used to warmth and tactile behaviour.' This figure was that feeling personified, with a big shot of classic teen angst. 'I think most teenagers feel crappy and like they're alone and nobody likes them', he said.

He didn't come up with much story beyond that. That came from writer Caroline Thompson. Thompson had written a novel, *First Born*, about an aborted foetus that comes back to life. She and Burton shared the same agent, who put them in touch, thinking they had similar outlooks. When they met, some time in early 1987, Burton told her about this weird drawing he had done of a guy with scissor hands. 'I said, "Stop right there. I know exactly what to do with that", and went home', remembered Thompson.

She came back to him a few days later with a full outline of the story, written like a novel, not a script. A kindly door-to-door saleswoman, Peg, discovers Edward, an odd, scissor-handed young man in a seemingly abandoned house on the edge of her typical suburban town. She invites him to come and live with her family. They warm to Edward, especially teenage daughter Kim, who develops feelings for him, but after initial fascination, the locals start to fear Edward. When he refuses to act like the novelty they want him to be, they turn on him and chase him out of town.

All the main characters were based on people from Thompson's life. Peg and her husband, Bill, were her parents; Kim her teenage best friend. It was exactly what Burton wanted, a suburban

BELOW: Peg (Dianne Wiest), the woman who brings the isolated Edward (Johnny Depp) into the big wide world.

fairytale retelling of *Frankenstein*, 'where the creature was the one that was most tormented, but also the one with the most heart'.

The story of Johnny Depp's casting as Edward is a well-worn Hollywood legend. Burton saw many big-name actors for the role, including Tom Cruise, Gary Oldman and Tom Hanks, but mostly out of politeness and studio insistence. He always knew he wanted Depp. He's never been quite sure exactly where he first spotted him. He hadn't seen *21 Jump Street*, a teen TV show Depp was starring in and desperate to get out of. He'd just seen his face somewhere and thought this man was Edward. As soon as they met, Burton's instinct was validated. 'There is this perception of [Johnny] as a teen idol, but he's really not that person', said Burton. 'That's just how he was perceived by society, and thus who he was. That's exactly like Edward. The studio wasn't immediately convinced about hiring a barely known actor, but Burton got his way. It was the beginning of one of the most fruitful pairings in cinema history.

It's hard to overstate the bravery of Depp's performance in *Edward Scissorhands*. It could so easily have gone horribly wrong. Look at his introduction, emerging from the shadows in a creepy old house, shuffling nervously forward with his bladed hands. It could have been career-endingly ridiculous. Instead, thanks to the clear trust between director and star, it remains one of the best performances of Depp's career. For the first two weeks, Depp was certain he was overdoing it. 'I just thought, "There's no way I can get away with this." But luckily, Tim was happy', he said. Burton was *so* happy that, according to an interview he gave many years later, his own view of *Edward Scissorhands* evolved thanks to Depp. Initially, the film was shaped by Burton's memories of growing up

RIGHT: Winona Ryder as Kim. Ryder and Depp were already a real-life couple when they began filming.

CHAPTER FOUR

feeling misunderstood. The more he watched Depp, the more it became about his experience as a reluctant celebrity. 'It turned into more my perception of [Johnny], in a way,' he said, 'what he goes through, how he's perceived, than it did even myself.'

Burton surrounded Depp with a more experienced cast. Dianne Wiest and Alan Arkin were cast as Peg and Bill, and Winona Ryder, by then an established star (and also Depp's girlfriend), was Kim, marking her second collaboration with Burton.

Edward Scissorhands is the first Burton film developed from one of his original ideas, and it's the work of a director who knows just who he is. He is there in every detail. Peg's hometown, with its identikit ice cream-coloured houses, with interiors devoid of personality, is a stylized version of the Burbank streets of Burton's youth. The architectural haircuts Edward gives to the women of the town look like Burton drawings. And in that eerie, twisted house on the hill, there lives, for a few moments, a tribute to the films that inspired Burton, and a little gift to himself.

Ever since Vincent Price had provided the voiceover for Burton's short film *Vincent*, the pair had maintained a friendship. Burton wrote the role of Edward's father/creator specifically for Price. Price only appears for a few minutes, shown building Edward and teaching him how to behave in society, then dying just before he gives Edward his hands. Playing Edward's creator would, though nobody knew it at the time, be Price's last film role, and it's a beautiful note on which to close his career. It's heartfelt, offering a nod to his horror past guided by someone who treasured him.

Although it wasn't a commercial hit at the time, affection for *Edward Scissorhands* has grown over the years. It brought Burton the best reviews of his career so far and made many people who had dismissed him as just a talented visualist view him as a true filmmaker. And it was as much proof to himself as to the rest of the world. 'Before I started directing, I barely spoke', Burton once said. 'That was what *Edward Scissorhands* was about: having a lot of feelings but not being able to project them.' On this film, he had truly found his voice.

A Visit With Vincent

While shooting *Edward Scissorhands*, Burton asked Vincent Price, who played Edward's creator, if he wouldn't mind sitting for an interview about his life and career. Burton had been devoted to Price since he was a child. He once said that Price's films, which typically saw him playing tormented characters, 'helped me get through life'.

Price agreed to the interview and he and Burton talked over three days. The film, which was initially going to be called *Conversations With Vincent* and later changed to *A Visit With Vincent*, was put on hold when Burton committed to directing *Batman Returns* in 1992. Price died in 1993 and, though there was some talk of Burton finishing the film in the mid-90s, it has never been completed.

*'Visions are worth fighting for.
Why spend your life making
someone else's dreams?'*

THE
GOLDEN
AGE

BATMAN RETURNS
1992

In the modern blockbuster industry, it would be madness to launch a big-budget film without plans for a sequel. Franchises and 'universes' are now the thing. But they didn't really exist in the early 1990s. Sequels were made if a film did especially well, but they were rarely, if ever, planned in advance. When Tim Burton was asked to make a sequel to *Batman*, he was almost shocked.

Burton had never really considered the possibility of a second Batman film, and when Warner Bros asked him to direct it, he initially said no. 'I don't like sequels', he said. 'They usually take what worked on the first movie and jack it up, making more of the same.' As pleased as he was with *Batman*, he didn't love the experience of a studio telling him what to do. After considerable freedom on *Pee-wee* and *Beetlejuice*, making a film with executives peering over his shoulder wasn't something Burton was desperate to repeat. He said yes on one condition: he was going to do everything his way. And that's almost what he got. 'There was definitely more freedom, in a certain way', he said. 'There's never freedom on a big film, but it was a different energy that way, definitely.'

If *Batman* is perhaps more structurally sound than its sequel, *Batman Returns* feels more true to Burton. It's even more enamoured of its characters' misfit natures and has something of a fairytale mood. It isn't entirely accurate to call it a sequel. Other than a passing mention of Bruce Wayne's 'ex-girlfriend' Vicki Vale, there's minimal connective tissue between this and the first film.

'They all have psychological problems, these characters', said Burton. 'I could relate to them much more than any other comic book character.' For *Batman Returns*, Burton gave Batman two foes: Oswald Cobblepot/the Penguin and Selina Kyle/Catwoman.

First, we're introduced to Cobblepot, dropped into Gotham's sewers as a baby because he's born with deformities that give him a beak-like nose and flipper hands. After 33 years living in hiding, he wants to return to public life. Cobblepot has spent his decades sifting through the secrets the city flushes down the toilet, which has given him plenty of material to blackmail corrupt businessman Max Shreck (Christopher Walken), the most powerful man in Gotham. Cobblepot forces Shreck to use his influence to help him run for mayor. Selina Kyle (Michelle Pfeiffer), Shreck's mousey personal assistant, foolishly reveals her knowledge of her boss's shady practices and gets pushed out of a window for her troubles. Resurrected by stray felines, she reinvents herself as Catwoman, setting her sights on revenge. She enters into a tricky relationship with Bruce Wayne, played once more by Michael Keaton.

This time, Burton had actors lining up to be his villains. Casting Oswald Cobblepot was fairly straightforward. In an early draft of the script, by *Batman* screenwriter Sam Hamm, the Penguin character was more human-looking. Dustin Hoffman, Christopher

RIGHT: Danny DeVito as Oswald Cobblepot, aka the Penguin. The actor stayed in character throughout shooting.

ABOVE: Michelle Pfeiffer had to be sewn into Catwoman's skin-tight outfit every day.

Lloyd and Robert De Niro were all in the running at that point. However, Burton nixed that script and a new one was written by Daniel Waters (*Heathers*; 1988). In Waters' vision, which Burton loved, Penguin became a sewer-dwelling, vertically-challenged outcast. From that point, only Danny DeVito was considered.

Finding Catwoman was a more protracted process. Burton cast Annette Bening, but she became pregnant and had to drop out. Many stars, including Cher, Susan Sarandon and Madonna, reportedly vied for the role. Michelle Pfeiffer had a subtler plan. A fan of Catwoman since childhood, she'd been devastated when she learned Bening had been cast. She had friends on the production and wasn't afraid to use her connections. 'I asked

ABOVE: Selina (Michelle Pfeiffer) and Bruce (Michael Keaton) learn each other's real identities at the masked ball.

them to *beg* Tim Burton to write me one scene', she said. 'I said I would do it for free.' There was no need. Even though Burton was only aware of her from *Scarface* (1983) he and Pfeiffer met and got on immediately. He didn't even make her audition. She was his Catwoman, and she became arguably the most iconic incarnation of the character.

Pfeiffer studied hard to become an expert with a whip. That scene where she thwacks heads off the mannequins was all her, in one take. For Selina's feline resurrection sequence, she let cats chew on her fingers and claw at her face. In one scene, she held a live bird in her mouth for more than 20 seconds before letting it fly out. 'She was, like, 100 per cent', said Burton.

ABOVE: Villainous businessman Max Shreck (Christopher Walken), after pushing his assistant Selina out of the window.

Batman Returns faced some criticism that it was barely a Batman film, instead focusing much more on the villains. This is broadly true. It's almost 15 minutes before Bruce Wayne makes an appearance, and close to 40 before he actually speaks a line, which was partly down to Keaton. In a gesture almost unheard of for actors, he asked for a huge chunk of his lines to be cut. 'He wanted to have very minimal dialogue, especially in the Batsuit', said screenwriter Daniel Waters. As Keaton had told Jack Nicholson on the set of the first film, Batman should be able to communicate without words: 'You gotta *work the suit*, man'. And he did.

This could be seen as more Catwoman's movie. It's her arc we're most focused on, from meek victim to ruler of her own destiny. 'That's my favourite character', said Burton many years later. Selina Kyle offers him so much, neither hero nor villain, and not interested in defining herself. Pfeiffer is effectively playing three parts: early innocent Selina; post transformation vamp Selina; and Catwoman. If you want to be pseudy about it, *Batman Returns* is about three different responses to rejection: Bruce Wayne wants to be loved and tries to find that acceptance by doing good for people; Penguin tries to demand attention by tricking and blackmailing people; and Catwoman decides life isn't worth wasting trying to make anyone like you. Hers is the most interesting take.

The setting even seems designed for Catwoman this time. Where the first film was all muscular architecture and shadowy alleys, the sequel takes place under an almost permanent blanket of snow, all the better for creeping around in catlike silence. While all those snowy scenes look beautiful, the sets caused some trouble for the cast. Though none of the snow was real, it was a chilly experience for Pfeiffer, who spends most of the film in skin-tight latex. And, while she loved playing Catwoman, the costume was an ordeal.

Every day, Pfeiffer would have to be powdered from head to toe and heaved into the suit by several dressers. Once she started moving around, vacuums would form around her joints, making it hard to move. To add indignity, the costume designers initially neglected to provide any way for her to exit the suit swiftly should nature call. Because several members of Penguin's entourage were played by actual penguins, sets frequently had to be chilled to a temperature comfortable for them. Pfeiffer was one cold kitty. Still, she considered herself lucky compared to DeVito in padding and prosthetics: 'I'd rather be cold in a rubber suit than have stuff glued to my face'.

DeVito didn't especially mind the stuff glued to his face, because at least he was warm. 'I was the only one really comfortable, because I had pounds and pounds of face prosthetics and the body padding', he said. And according to Walken, the real DeVito never emerged from under that padding. He stayed in character throughout. 'Once he was in that costume, he was the Penguin', he said. 'I saw Danny after the movie, never during production.'

Batman Returns wasn't nearly as successful as the first film, making $268 million to *Batman*'s $411 million. Although Warner Bros didn't give Burton total carte blanche, he had made primarily the film he wanted to make, and that wasn't necessarily the film the studio wanted to sell. There's a level of sexuality that's higher than is typical for a superhero movie. At one point, Catwoman gropes Batman. And Penguin goes into some sort of grunting fit over seeing Catwoman in her suit. It's also quite violent. In the first major action sequence, Batman sets a circus performer on fire, breaking the superhero's traditional rule of not deliberately killing anyone. And the finale sees Catwoman kill Max Schreck with an electrified kiss. This isn't a film for children.

After his reluctance to return, Burton was up for a third film. He had plenty of ideas. He wanted to bring in Robin, and had in fact cast Marlon Wayans in the role in *Batman Returns*, before cutting him because the cast was too swollen (Wayans has said he still gets residual cheques). He also considered a Catwoman spin-off, which Daniel Waters said would have been 'an $18 million black-and-white movie'. Pfeiffer was keen but said discussions 'didn't last very long'.

Ultimately, however, this time it was Warner Bros who decided to move on. Burton met with the studio about a third movie and was confused by the executives in the room repeatedly suggesting other films he might like to make. 'I realized halfway through my meeting. . .that they didn't really want me to do the movie', he said. So, Warner Bros gave directing duties to the lighter, brighter Joel Schumacher and Burton said so long to Gotham.

BELOW: Batman (Michael Keaton) faces off against the Penguin's minions.

THE NIGHTMARE BEFORE CHRISTMAS
1993

Burton was always much more one for drawing than writing, but after completing his short film *Vincent*, in 1982, he wrote a little poem, combining his two favourite holidays, Christmas and Halloween. To the rhythm of 'Twas the Night Before Christmas', 'The Nightmare Before Christmas' told of Jack Skellington, an inhabitant of the spooky Halloweenland who is fed up with ghosts and ghouls and dreams of something new. When he takes a wrong turn in a forest and finds himself in the snowy, jolly Christmas Town, Jack decides that this is what he wants: a new holiday to celebrate. So he steals Christmas and kidnaps Santa Claus.

'Every Christmas you'd watch those stories like *Rudolph the Red-Nosed Reindeer* (1964) or *How the Grinch Stole Christmas* (1966)', said Burton. 'Those were my favourite holiday specials growing up. So, when I was working at Disney, I designed something that's like the reverse of that. Like *The Grinch* in reverse, about this character who finds Christmas and loves it and tries to do it himself.' Burton sketched out ideas for the characters and the look of the world. He had his friend Rick Heinrichs make a sculpture of

Jack Skellington. Jack, who looks like a nightmare but is a total innocent, is a classic Burton hero. 'It was based on those feelings growing up of people perceiving you as something dark or weird when actually you're not', said Burton.

He had ideas about possibly turning the story into a TV special, but when he left Disney, it sat untouched for years. By the start of the 1990s, however, it would be dusted off. Burton was going back to the studio that fired him the previous decade, and *The Nightmare Before Christmas* would become the best Tim Burton movie Tim Burton never made.

Burton didn't direct *The Nightmare Before Christmas*, but the man who did, Henry Selick, so fully captures the Burton aesthetic and mood that many assume it's Burton's work. Burton and Selick knew each other from their time at Disney, where, said Selick, 'We bonded, because we weren't the typical Disney people.' Since leaving Disney, Selick was a jobbing animator, with some experience in stop-motion. When, in 1991, he got a call from Rick Heinrichs asking if he wanted to meet about making a *Nightmare* movie, Selick was shocked. Not just because Burton wasn't making it himself – Burton was already committed to directing *Batman Returns* – but because a studio was willing to make a stop-motion-animated feature at all.

At the time, Disney was in the thick of a golden age of animation. *Who Framed Roger Rabbit* (1988) had pushed the boundaries of the genre a few years previously and it was feeling very confident in its latest feature, *Beauty and the Beast* (1991), which would go on to become the first animated movie nominated for a Best Picture Oscar. The studio thought a prestige stop-motion film would further show its dominance in animation.

Burton and Danny Elfman had been working on the film for some time when Selick came aboard. The songs were written

ABOVE: Jack (whose speaking voice is provided by Chris Sarandon) gives a child a very unmerry Christmas.

before anything else, blocking out the shape of the film and Jack's arc. In tunes like 'Jack's Lament' and 'What's This?', Jack is shown to be a leader who is tired of his lot and yearns for something more. Something tinselly.

The songs would provide the spine of the story, then Caroline Thompson, writer of *Edward Scissorhands*, was hired to write a screenplay around them. She built on Burton's original poem, but didn't alter it too much. Halloweenland became Halloween Town. The character of Sally, a Bride of Frankenstein-ish doll who's desperate to escape her dull life, was expanded into a co-lead. The overall story, though, is much as it was when Burton wrote it in 1982.

By October 1991, animation had begun in San Francisco. Some 230 sets were constructed across nine soundstages. More than 100 creatives were employed, with the animation carried out by just 13. Every second of animation requires 24 frames, each minutely adjusted from the last. To give an idea of how painstaking the process is, Jack Skellington alone had at least 300 different facial expressions. It isn't surprising it took two years. And this wasn't the low-tech stop-motion of Ray Harryhausen's era. *The Nightmare Before Christmas* employed some cutting-edge technology to make it look more spectacular than any stop-motion that had come before.

Stop-motion animation traditionally had a rudimentary, televisual look, because the camera had to be kept in a single position while the animators worked; animating with a moving camera was virtually impossible. On *Nightmare*, director of photography Pete Kozachik developed technology that would allow for grand, sweeping camera moves that could follow the rhythms of a song and make everything look more 'cinematic'. Before any animation started, the camera moves were planned, then programmed into a computer. The computer moved the camera a fractional amount for every frame. This transformed the possibilities of the movie. Watch the

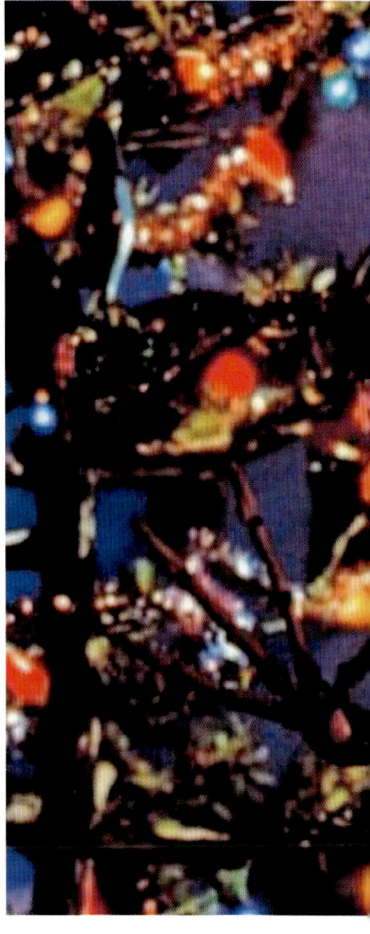

ABOVE: Jack Skellington discovers the joys of Christmas Town.

opening number, 'This is Halloween', and the camera is almost constantly moving. That had never been possible before.

For all the studio's bravado about showing its commitment to breaking new ground in stop-motion animation, Disney became nervous when it came time to actually release *Nightmare*. '[It's] stop-motion, the main character doesn't have any eyeballs and it's all music, what's to feel comfortable about?', said Burton.

Disney was worried the film was too scary for children and released it not under the Disney banner, but under that of its more 'adult' subsidiary, Touchstone Pictures. 'They thought it could damage the brand', said Selick. But, as Burton always knew, you should never underestimate children's enthusiasm for dark stories. *Nightmare* earned mostly positive reviews and became a modest success on its original release (around $80 million worldwide, on an $18 million budget). It has grown into a festive classic, re-released in cinemas multiple times over the years and

James and the Giant Peach

Three years after the release of *The Nightmare Before Christmas*, Burton produced Henry Selick's take on Roald Dahl's *James and the Giant Peach*, A stop-motion/live-action hybrid, it tells of a boy who travels the world inside an enormous peach filled with an insect crew.

The look is distinctly Burtonesque, even down to a character, Miss Spider, having the signature Burton black-and-white stripes. Jack Skellington even makes an uncredited cameo, as the captain of a pirate ship.

celebrated at live concerts of its music. It's earned vastly more money than its original theatrical run, not least through a huge amount of merchandise. You can barely move for Skellington merch when Halloween comes around. It has earned a place in the hearts of generations of audiences. Jack Skellington is not just for Christmas. At least, not just for *one* Christmas.

BELOW: Catherine O'Hara, who played Delia in *Beetlejuice*, reunited with Burton to voice Sally.

ED WOOD
1994

Edward D Wood Jr was, in his way, the director Tim Burton dreamed of being. Prolific in the 1950s, Wood made movies that include *Bride of the Monster* (1955), *Plan 9 From Outer Space* (1957) and *Night of the Ghouls* (1959). He made films exactly as he wanted to make them. He always believed in himself, no matter how many knockbacks he got. Some considered his behaviour weird, but he didn't listen. The fact that Wood was considered *dreadful* at making films didn't deter Burton. Quite the opposite. He knew a thing or two about forging on in the face of critical derision.

The general public gave Wood little thought when he was alive. He only really gained notoriety in 1980, two years after his death, when he was named The Worst Director in History in a book called *The Golden Turkey Awards*, by Harry and Michael Medved. It was a title bestowed by two men, not a public vote, but the label stuck and film-loving audiences started to take an ironic interest in Wood.

Burton was aware of Wood, but no superfan or scholar. He had seen, and unironically enjoyed, *Plan 9 From Outer Space* as a kid and knew of Wood's growing following. After finishing *Batman Returns,* he was struggling to settle on his next project. He was originally only going to produce an Ed Wood film, to be written by Scott Alexander and Larry Karaszewski, but the more he researched Wood, the more he was drawn to him. He decided he wanted to make this film himself, which would be a celebration of a man's inextinguishable enthusiasm for filmmaking and determination never to give up.

'It's a fine line between failure and success', said Burton. 'To be known as the worst, at least you're known for something. That beautiful passion [Wood has] as a filmmaker. When he was making *Plan 9*, he thought he was making *Star Wars*. . .Except for the women's clothing angle, I completely related to him.' The women's clothing angle refers to Wood's love of cross-dressing. In *Glen or Glenda* (1953) he plays a man with a secret love of women's clothing. Wood had a particular affinity for angora sweaters.

If Burton thought his proven box-office success would earn him favour in Hollywood, he was wrong. Even though *Ed Wood* cost just $18 million and Burton took a huge pay cut to direct, it was a struggle to get it made. He ultimately wound up at Disney, after other studios rejected it. There was some apprehension about Burton making the film in black and white, which he insisted on because it suited the period and it would look odd to recreate Wood's films in colour. And he didn't want to fill it with big-name stars.

Wood, like Burton, had a troupe of actors, who he took from film to film. Burton cast some names, including Bill Murray as gender-fluid Bunny Breckinridge, but most were unknowns, such as Lisa Marie as Morticiaesque TV personality Vampira and wrestler George 'The Animal' Steele as wrestler Tor. One piece of casting he got no pushback on, following the success of *Edward Scissorhands*, was Johnny Depp as Wood. 'He called me one night and whispered,

BELOW: Johnny Depp as Ed Wood as Glen in *Glen Or Glenda*.

"Johnny, can you meet me at the Formosa Café?"', said Depp. 'I felt like I was in a spy story. I got there, had a beer, and within ten minutes I'd said yes.'

It's a gift of a part for Depp, who at this point still wasn't getting such big chewy roles elsewhere. He seized on it with what would become characteristic zeal, deciding that Wood's personality would be a combination of the 'blind optimism and enthusiasm' of Ronald Reagan, the 'salesman quality' of American DJ Casey Kasem and 'the Tin Man from *Wizard of Oz*'. His performance was proof that he and Burton were a magical combination. Depp will do anything for him. In one memorable scene, Wood performs a striptease for his film crew, in full Glenda get-up. It's staged in a way that's celebratory of Wood, not making fun of him. There are not many big-name actors who'd have done that in the 90s.

The film follows a fairly traditional biopic structure. We meet Wood as he's trying to get a foothold in Hollywood. When he manages to persuade a crummy producer, who puts out cheap horror and skin flicks, to let him direct *Glen or Glenda*, it looks as if Wood is on his way. The gag is that success eternally evades Wood, due to his complete lack of talent, but he just keeps trying. He begs and cajoles his way to making film after film, each as bad as the last, his enthusiasm rarely dimmed. 'I was fascinated by the weird, perverted optimism because it's something that I started out with and has somewhat eroded', said Burton at the time of the film's release. '[*Ed Wood*] kind of re-energized me.'

There's a running joke about Wood comparing himself to Orson Welles, considered one of history's *best* movie directors. In one of the film's final scenes, Wood, in angora sweater and heels, bumps into Welles in a bar and chats to him like a contemporary, bemoaning interfering producers and wondering if it's all worth it. 'Ed,' Welles tells him, 'visions are worth fighting for. Why spend your life making someone else's dreams?' It's a wholly fictional encounter, but it

ABOVE: Ed (Johnny Depp) and Bela Lugosi (Martin Landau). Landau won an Oscar for his role.

states exactly how Wood and Burton feel about movies. Sometimes the process sucks, but if you are going to do it, do it for you.

The heart of *Ed Wood* is the friendship between Wood and Bela Lugosi. The latter became hugely famous in the 1930s for his horror movie appearances, primarily 1931's *Dracula*, but by the 1960s he was struggling for work and addicted to morphine, which he initially took to ease his sciatica. Wood, a huge fan, befriended Lugosi and persuaded him to appear in several of his movies, including *Glen or Glenda* and *Plan 9 From Outer Space*. Burton saw parallels with a friendship of his own.

ABOVE: Bill Murray as John 'Bunny' Breckinridge, who played The Ruler in Ed Wood's *Plan 9 From Outer Space.*

'His relationship with Bela Lugosi reminded me of the feeling I remember having with Vincent Price', he said. Burton had looked up to Price since childhood and eventually befriended him. They had worked together on the short film *Vincent* and *Edward Scissorhands* and stayed very close until Price died in 1993. Of course, Wood and Lugosi's friendship wasn't at all similar in the specifics, but Burton could relate to getting to know your hero as a mortal.

Lugosi is played by Martin Landau, Burton's only choice for the role. He plays him beautifully, as someone who's just as impassioned about film as Wood, but without the optimism. Lugosi knows his star has faded and is thrilled at the possibility of another moment in the spotlight, even as repeated disappointment and addiction drag him down. Landau won a Best Supporting Actor Oscar for the role.

Making *Ed Wood* was, in almost all respects, a happy experience for Burton. It brought some of the most glowing reviews of his career. Deservedly so, as it remains one of his best. Compared to many of his films, it's very minimalist, with simple framing and no visual eccentricities. He isn't directing in the style of Ed Wood – he's far too good for that – but restricts himself to a lot of the same toolkit. Like Wood, he had no money for fancy production techniques. It's very effective.

There was a small cloud of sadness hanging over *Ed Wood*. After an unbroken run since *Pee-wee's Big Adventure*, this is the first Burton film that isn't scored by Danny Elfman. Elfman said 'a falling out is inevitable' when you work together for as long, and as closely, as he and Burton. They had gone from *Batman* to *Edward Scissorhands* to *Batman Returns* in the space of three years, while Elfman was simultaneously writing the score and lyrics for *The Nightmare Before Christmas*. He was worn out and something had to give. There was no specific issue that caused the catastrophic argument, but it was enough to shatter their friendship. 'We used to joke that we'd end up like Bernard Herrmann and Alfred Hitchcock, who had this massive blow-up that they never reconciled', said Elfman. 'Then there we were, in fact, having that exact same thing.' *Ed Wood* was scored by Howard Shore.

A year later, both Burton and Elfman felt terrible about their falling out. Elfman got a call from someone close to Burton to ask if he would ever consider working with him again. The next day, he was on a plane to Kansas for a reunion. Burton greeted him with a big hug and said, 'That was awful. Let's not even speak of it'. So, they didn't but jumped into the next project. And they haven't fallen out again since.

*'Damn them. . .
damn them all to hell!'*

A DIRECTOR IN FLUX

MARS ATTACKS!
1996

'That was my Ed Wood movie!' was how Tim Burton once jokingly described this follow-up to his Wood biopic. Which isn't to say he considers *Mars Attacks!* a terrible movie, but that it's the sort of simple, campy, logic-be-damned sci-fi Wood used to try to make. It's Burton's take on the alien pictures of the 1950s and 1960s. 'I wanted to do something fun with a bunch of Martians with big brains', he said. 'Basically, make a modern version of *Plan 9 From Outer Space* or *The War of the Worlds*.' It sits somewhere between the two on the scale of silliness.

Mars Attacks! is based on a series of illustrated trading cards, originally released by Topps in the 1960s, depicting green-faced, mega-brained Martians zapping humans to bits with ray guns. There's no story to the series, just a lot of garish extraterrestrial destruction. The idea for the movie came up in 1994, when Burton was spitballing with Thomas Lassally, a Warner Bros executive. Burton was waxing nostalgic about the *Dinosaurs Attack* card series he used to love, in which dinosaurs came back to life to kill humans. Steven Spielberg's *Jurassic Park* (1993) had come out

ABOVE: Art (Jack Nicholson) and Barbara Land (Annette Bening) before the Martians come calling.

the year earlier, so that idea was a no-go for adaptation, but it made Lassally remember the *Mars Attacks!* cards. Burton called the next day to say he wanted to make a movie based on them.

Mars Attacks! makes more sense once you know it's based on trading cards, because that's sort of how it plays, as a bunch of small, daffy ideas shuffled together. Burton said he and writer Jonathan Gems approached it like an animated movie: 'Just kick around some ideas and thoughts and draft the screenplay that way'. Gems had never had a screenplay actually produced, but had worked on an aborted sequel to *Beetlejuice*, so he and Burton had a connection. As they developed the idea, over viewings of cheesy old sci-fi movies, they decided they wanted to combine aliens with the disaster movies of the 1970s – *Towering Inferno, The Poseidon Adventure, Airport* – but make it comedic. They piled up ridiculous concepts. Gems was briefly fired from the project by Warner Bros for refusing to remove an opening sequence of flaming cows running over a hill, even though it was taken directly from a card. Gems was replaced by *Ed Wood* writers Larry Karaszewski and Scott Alexander, but rejoined at a later date and has sole screenwriting credit. His flaming cows made it into the movie.

The resulting film doesn't try to expand on the premise offered by the trading cards. Its plot is simply that Martians come to Earth, in flying saucers that look very much like props from *Ed Wood*, with the intention of destroying its inhabitants. No deeper motivation is offered. The fun, then, is in the huge cast of characters who find themselves in the aliens' way. And it's a *huge* cast. Early drafts had been budgeted at $280 million, which was never going to happen, but even when it was brought down to $70 million, there was no way it could be made without everyone taking a huge pay cut. All the main cast except one were paid the same: $100,000 per week.

Only Jack Nicholson was paid more, but in fairness, he's playing two roles. Nicholson plays the US president, who's trying, with minimal success or strategy, to lead his country through uncharted territory and make peace with the visitors. Glenn Close plays his wife, Natalie Portman his daughter, Martin Short his press secretary and Rod Steiger his head of military. Nicholson's other role is casino-owner Art Land. A quick sketch of a character, he seems to be just an excuse to set some of the film in the bright lights and kitsch of Las Vegas. Art is married to hippie Barbara (Annette Bening, getting a chance to work with Burton after missing out on playing Catwoman in *Batman Returns*). Inhabitants of Art's casino include Danny DeVito as a gambler and singer Tom Jones as himself. Elsewhere, Sarah Jessica Parker and Michael J Fox play TV presenters covering the invasion; Lukas Haas is a young man who

ABOVE: Lisa Marie as a Martian in disguise, ready to break into the White House.

lives in a trailer with his family, including Christina Applegate and a pre-fame Jack Black, and is racing across the country to rescue his grandmother, Sylvia Sidney; Pierce Brosnan is a smarmy scientist who purports to understand the Martians; and Pam Grier is a bus driver trying to keep her kids safe. That isn't even close to the whole cast, which goes some way to explaining why it's a challenge to keep track of who's who and what they're doing. Many of the characters get just a few minutes on screen. Then, of course, there are all the Martians.

ABOVE: Jack Nicholson in his second role in the movie, as US President James Dale.

In 1996, CGI was still a novelty. Three years earlier, *Jurassic Park* had shown what could be done by the best technicians in the business, but Burton was distrustful of computer imagery and wanted to bring the aliens to life with stop-motion. He went as far as employing teams to do months of stop-motion animation tests, until the studio put a stop to it. The effects, by Industrial Light & Magic (ILM), who brought *Jurassic Park*'s dinosaurs to life, are one of the most impressive parts of the movie. Pretty much recreating the alien look from the cards, the Martians look convincingly real yet simultaneously a little awkward, with some of the jerkiness of Ray Harryhausen's stop-motion work.

It's a great-looking film. Production designer Wynn Thomas had just come off the drag queen comedy *To Wong Foo, Thanks For Everything!, Julie Newmar* (1995), and brought a heavy dose of camp with him. All its most memorable moments are almost purely visual. The best features Burton's then-girlfriend, Lisa Marie, as a Martian disguised as a human woman. Or a Martian's impression of a human woman. With an absurdly pneumatic figure and giant hair (all the better to hide her huge Martian brain), she sweeps through the corridors of the White House, silently chewing gum and gliding along as if on a conveyor belt (because Lisa Marie was). As a piece of plot, it's near-pointless – the alien makes it into the heart of US power, thanks to Martin Short's horny press secretary, but then gets shot to bits – but it certainly looks cool. In another stand-out sequence, Sarah Jessica Parker's ditzy journalist, whose head has been chopped off and grafted onto the body of her pet chihuahua, romances the disembodied bonce of Pierce Brosnan's scientist. That image sort of sums up the daftness of the whole endeavour. There's no substance to it, but it's hard to truly dislike.

Audiences, however, stayed well away. It made less than $38 million in the United States, although it was more popular overseas. It was a blow to Burton, who had exhausted himself getting it made. When it flopped, he promised himself some time off. He even told Gems he might not 'ever make another movie again'. But he would be back a few years later, returning to his darker roots, with another tribute to a childhood favourite. This time with a lot more success.

RIGHT: Nathalie (Sarah Jessica Parker) with her dog, with whom she'll soon be very closely bonded.

SLEEPY HOLLOW
1999

For most of 1997, Tim Burton was deep in development on *Superman Lives*, which would have returned him to the superhero genre. It was a fraught process, and by early 1998, after many aborted takeoffs, the film was cancelled. Burton was simultaneously furious and despondent. 'I felt like I wasted a year, and that's the worst feeling you can have', he said. 'It was traumatic.'

His schedule suddenly open, Burton was handed a script that would put him back onto familiar ground and result in one of his most purely enjoyable, and visually beautiful, films. It was a story that Burton, like many Americans, knew very well.

Written in 1820, by Washington Irving, *The Legend of Sleepy Hollow* tells of Ichabod Crane, a gangly, superstitious schoolmaster who means to woo and marry the wealthy Katrina Van Tassel, but has competition in the form of the burly Brom. Trying to scare off his rival, Brom tells Ichabod the tale of the Headless Horseman, a soldier who was beheaded in the Revolutionary War and, at night, rides the lands around the village of Sleepy Hollow, searching for his lost skull. One night, Ichabod is chased by the Headless

Horseman and disappears, leaving Brom to marry Katrina. Just what happened to Ichabod is never revealed. It's a short story, with broad characters, but the shiver-inducing central conceit established it as an American classic. It memorably became a Disney animated short in 1949.

The script, credited to Andrew Kevin Walker (*Se7en*; 1995), but given an uncredited polish by Tom Stoppard (*Shakespeare in Love*; 1998), cleverly and hugely expands the slim fable. In this version, set in 1799, Ichabod Crane is a nervy police constable sent to Sleepy Hollow, which has been plagued by a spate of gruesome murders, each of the victims beheaded. The villagers insist it's the work of the Headless Horseman, but Ichabod, a man who believes in science over spirituality and superstition, is determined that there's a logical explanation. This is a gothic whodunnit with a shot of romance, as Ichabod grows close to Katrina Van Tassell, though doesn't make her exempt from his list of suspects.

The script had been sitting around for about six years before producer Scott Rudin (*The Addams Family*; 1991, *Clueless*; 1995) suggested it to Burton. It was just what he needed. 'I didn't want to make any old piece of crap just to move on – I didn't want to be like, "Okay, I'll do *Police Academy 8* because I need the work"', said Burton at the time. 'So when *Sleepy Hollow* was presented to me, it was like "This is the script". . .Maybe it was because of my previous year that I related to a character with no head.'

Burton's vision for the film took him back to the Hammer Horror movies he'd loved in his youth. *Sleepy Hollow* has the same kind of look and tone as *Dracula* (1958) and *The Devil Rides Out* (1968). The scenery has just a hint of pantomime and the acting is a little too big, deliberately. However, Burton never lets it slip into pastiche. The horror elements are genuinely unnerving and the entire production design deservedly won an Oscar for Rick Heinrichs.

Superman Doesn't Live

In 1998, after over a year of pre-production, Burton was three weeks away from starting shooting on *Superman Lives*. He had Nicolas Cage cast in the title role. He had scouted locations. It was to be his glorious return to the world of DC superheroes, a decade after *Batman*. It was cancelled at the eleventh hour, with Warner Bros fearing the film was going to be simply too expensive to make. *Batman & Robin* had underperformed the year before, making the studio nervous about blowing the budget on another comic book movie.

Burton's take on Superman would have leaned into the idea of Kal-El (Superman's birth name) as an alien on Earth. The latest script had Superman battling the super-intelligent villain Brainiac and almost being killed. He has a robot sidekick who turns into a mechanical suit when Superman loses his powers. It would also have done away with the traditional underpants-over-tights outfit.

Cage tried to resurrect the film for a while after Burton's departure, but it soon died. Superman was eventually reborn, without Cage, in 2006 with *Superman Returns*. The red underpants were revived.

Sleepy Hollow marks the third team-up between Burton and Johnny Depp, who plays Ichabod. At the time, Depp was considered one of the industry's best actors, but still not a great box-office draw. The studio, Paramount, tried to steer Burton towards more obviously commercial stars, like Brad Pitt. It would have been a very different film with Pitt. Depp plays Ichabod, in Burton's words, 'almost like a 13-year-old girl'. Ichabod is terrified of everything, flinching when Katrina (Christina Ricci) talks to him, running for cover at the slightest sign of danger, or fainting at the sight of blood. If it were entirely up to Depp, he would have made Ichabod even odder. At the start of shooting, Depp informed Burton that he would be taking inspiration from Angela Lansbury in the overripe 1972 adaptation of Agatha Christie's *Death on the Nile*. Burton had to dissuade Depp from a notion that Ichabod should have a large false nose and ears, like Disney's version of the character.

Shooting the film in the United Kingdom allowed Burton to fill the cast with British character actors, such as Michael Gambon, Richard Griffiths, Ian McDiarmid and Miranda Richardson. And Hammer's own Dracula, Christopher Lee, makes a cameo as a judge. They all get the tone completely. Watch each of their reactions as the Horseman (Christopher Walken when headed; Ray Park when headless) comes to claim them. They pitch it towards melodrama, screaming in wild-eyed panic, but never into full camp. All experienced theatre performers, they're playing to the audience but without winking too hard at them.

There's some of Burton's strongest action direction here. He has said that the final chase sequence in the Disney animation, in which the horseman hunts down the hapless Ichabod, is a favourite of his, and you can see the influence in his sequences, particularly the climactic, extended chase. It manages to be heart-in-your-mouth terrifying and funny at the same time. Moments like Ichabod finding himself backwards on the horseman's steed could have come right out of the cartoon.

Burton was keen to avoid using CGI wherever possible, so many of the effects are practical, with sculpted decapitated heads rolling around all over the place. However, doing things practically wasn't always, well, practical. After some experiments with big-shouldered costumes, it was decided the only way to make the Headless Horseman look convincing was to have stuntman/actor Ray Park (also known as Darth Maul from *Star*

RIGHT: Christina Ricci as Katrina Van Tassell, Ichabod's love interest and murder suspect.

ABOVE: The Horseman (Christopher Walken) shortly before he loses his beloved head.

TOP RIGHT: Ichabod Crane (Johnny Depp), a schoolmaster in the original book, becomes a nervy police constable.

Wars: The Phantom Menace; 1999) wear a blue hood while shooting the horseman's scenes, which was digitally erased in post-production. Effects houses ILM and Computer Film Company (CFC) had to behead the horseman in 300 shots.

Surprisingly, given the deliberate fakery of its gore, *Sleepy Hollow* was slapped with a restrictive R-rating in the United States, meaning anyone under 17 couldn't see it unaccompanied. It earned a reasonable $101 million on release, but reviews were generally warm. In many ways, *Sleepy Hollow* feels like an antidote to the messiness of *Mars Attacks!* Both are salutes to favourite parts of Burton's childhood, but where *Mars Attacks!* is almost mocking of terrible sci-fi movies, everything about *Sleepy Hollow* is brimming with love. It plainly adores all the high-concept plotting and scenery-chewing acting of the Hammer films it's echoing. This is Burton directing not with his head, but from his heart.

PLANET OF THE APES

2001

The opening weekend of *Planet of the Apes* thrilled 20th Century Fox. In its first few days, this huge budget remake brought in a record-breaking $68.5 million, more than any other film released that summer, beating the openings of *Jurassic Park III* and the $140-million giant *Pearl Harbor*. The gamble had paid off. Alas, it was also the film that nearly broke Tim Burton and earned a reputation as one of the worst blockbusters ever made.

Almost immediately after saying yes to directing, Burton had doubts. He was a huge fan of the original, and it's rarely a good idea to remake a classic. Considered one of the all-time great sci-fi movies, Franklin J Schaffner's 1968 film, based on Pierre Boulle's novel, sees a group of astronauts land on a strange planet, where humans are enslaved by apes. The big twist – arguably the best in any film ever – is that they have really landed on a future Earth, which was destroyed by nuclear war.

Schaffner's film spawned four sequels and two TV series through the 1970s. By the end of the 1980s, 20th Century Fox was trying to get a reboot off the ground, a journey that would take over a decade. It went across the desks of some of the industry's best filmmakers. Oliver Stone and James Cameron both had spells as potential producers. The Hughes brothers (*Menace II Society*; 1993) pitched a film that grappled with the theme of race in America. Roland Emmerich (*Independence Day*; 1996), Michael Bay (*Transformers*; 2007) and a then up-and-coming Peter Jackson all turned it down. Eventually, Burton was approached. At the time, his interest was piqued by the thought of putting a new spin on a story he loved. His film would be not a remake but a 're-imagining'. Things began to go wrong quickly.

Fox had a release date set before Burton came on board, so he was behind schedule before cameras had even started rolling. Added to that, the script Burton signed up for, by William Broyles Jr, was projected to cost at least $200 million. In an effort to bring costs down, Fox hired Lawrence Konner and Mark Rosenthal to do rushed rewrites. Burton remembers the film was only officially greenlit with about a week to go before filming.

LEFT: General Thade (Tim Roth) leads his army in an attempt to crush the human uprising.

Anyone watching the movie will probably not be surprised to learn that it started without a solid screenplay. From the first scenes, it's a confusing beast. It begins in space, in 2029, where a group of scientists, including Leo Davidson, are training chimps to pilot spacecraft. When one of those chimps disappears during an electromagnetic storm, Davidson heads after him. Lost in the storm, he crashes on a planet called Ashlar, in the year 5021. Ashlar is ruled by apes. Humans are considered their lowly servants. Davidson gradually becomes the head of a human uprising.

Mark Wahlberg, who had committed without reading a script because he wanted to work with Burton, plays Davidson. He, like Burton, had instant misgivings. 'The first day, I freaked out', he said. 'There was this kid with tribal markings on his face, a guy in a gorilla suit and Helena. It all seemed pretty ridiculous.' He wasn't wrong, but it isn't really the ape part that's ridiculous. The ape scenes are the ones that actually seem like a Tim Burton movie. It's the rest that's problematic.

Burton was lucky to have physical effects genius Rick Baker (*An American Werewolf in London*; 1981) designing the apes. Baker had been attached to the project for far longer than Burton, and the preparation shows. The apes – including Helena Bonham Carter (who plays the human-loving ape Ari), Tim Roth (as villainous General Thade), Michael Clark Duncan (as the head of Thade's army), and Paul Giamatti (as a comic-relief human-trader) – are stunningly created. All the actors had been through 'ape school' – Bonham Carter said the secret to a convincing chimp walk was to pretend you have 'a full nappy and don't want to spill it' – and Baker gave them prosthetics that were believably simian but also gave them the ability to emote. Their look is campy, sure, but appealingly so, and there's a level of charm to the scenes in the ape village, where chimpanzee kids play basketball and orangutans perform their morning ablutions hanging upside

ABOVE: Mark Wahlberg plays Captain Leo Davidson, an astronaut who crashes on the ape planet, Ashlar.

down. This was what Burton wanted. Always a lover of practical effects over digital, he was aiming for a modernized version of the original film's ape make-up. And that's what he got.

The humans are the bigger issue. The weight of carrying the story was put on the backs of Wahlberg and Estella Warren, an inexperienced actor playing Daena, one of Ashlar's native humans. Wahlberg has grown into a great action star, but he's not convincing as a scientist and looks lost in many scenes. Hardly his fault, given the ever-changing script. The story was being redrafted all the time and the actors didn't always know what was happening in any given scene. Wahlberg remembers watching the film and being confused by a moment when Ari begins to cry listening to Davidson and Daena talking about nothing especially important, 'I'm like, "What's wrong? What's going on?"'

ABOVE: Daena (Estella Warren) and Birn (Luke Eberl) prepare for battle.

Burton was no stranger to difficult shoots. His first blockbuster, *Batman*, had undergone significant rewrites while shooting, and that turned out well for everyone. He thought he would be able to do it again, but the difference on *Batman* was that he'd started shooting with a script he loved and understood. On *Apes*, he was trying to repair, at speed, something that had always been broken.

It wasn't an entirely unhappy shoot. Giamatti said Burton, 'made it not feel like a giant studio movie. He made it very intimate and fun'. Burton spoke positively of his experience with the actors and got a big kick out of Baker's work. It was also the film where he met Helena Bonham Carter, who would later become his partner and mother of his two children.

If Burton didn't manage to salvage *Apes,* it wasn't for want of effort. He shot it in 80 days, quite brief for a film of that size, and edited in just three months, which is almost unheard of for a blockbuster. His ape action scenes are pacey and fun, with chimps running on all fours and leaping through the trees, but the plot is incoherent and the characters all thin. Reviews ranged from middling to savage, with much ire reserved for the film's left-field ending. After an already far-fetched conclusion, in which the lost ape from Davidson's ship appears on Ashlar in a space pod, enabling Davidson to head back home, the story flies off the rails.

Burton knew audiences would expect a twist, but how do you out-twist the original? What they came up with is so confusing that its precise logic has been debated ever since. When Davidson arrives back on Earth, crashing in Washington, DC, he discovers the whole place is overrun by apes, with the statue that was once Abraham Lincoln now bearing the face of Thade. The broadly accepted theory of how that can be seems to be that after Davidson leaves Ashlar, Thade eventually, somehow frees himself from imprisonment, retrieves the second pod from the bottom of a lake and works out how to fly it back to Earth. . .to a time long before Davidson's arrival, enabling apes to evolve into the planet's dominant species.

This raises far more questions than it answers, not least, how did Thade figure out rocket science and why does ape-Earth have the same Washington monuments as our world? Burton has resisted talking about the film in the years since, although at the time he was happy to make his feelings clear. During press interviews, which are meant to be used to advertise a film, Burton was asked if he'd return for a sequel. 'I'd rather jump out the window,' he said, 'I swear to God.'

'Every day a new adventure, that's my motto'

THE
COMEBACK

BIG FISH
2003

In 1989, as part of a *New York Times* feature on the making of *Batman,* Joe Morgenstern interviewed Tim Burton's parents, Jean and Bill. While expressing how immensely proud they were of everything their son had achieved, they admitted their relationship with him wasn't close. 'I know he feels there were painful conflicts between us', said Jean. 'I think they were all from within [him].' Bill couldn't even bring himself to talk about why they rarely spoke. He didn't know the answer.

In the few interviews in which he has discussed them, Burton indicated he'd never been close to his parents, nor his younger brother, Daniel. He had 'an incredible desire to get out of the house from an early age.' But whatever your relationship with your parents, the loss of them reshapes you. Burton's father died in 2000, while Burton was in pre-production on *Planet of the Apes*. His mother died two years later. *Big Fish* is Burton's attempt to grapple with everything he felt.

Daniel Wallace's 1998 novel *Big Fish: A Novel of Mythic Proportions* is a beautiful book, full of evocative imagery, but not one that

BELOW: Under heavy prosthetics, Helena Bonham Carter plays the future-seeing witch.

easily lends itself to screen adaptation. It's about a man sitting at his father's deathbed, fearful that he has never truly known him and now it's too late. His dad has always told fanciful stories of his life, about adventures with giants and witches, and his son is frustrated by what he considers unhelpful lies. As he recounts his tales, the man begins to realize his father was telling him who he was all along, but trying to do it in a way that made a regular life sound more thrilling. He didn't want to be seen as the ordinary door-to-door salesman he was, just another minnow in the stream. He wanted to be a big fish.

Before the book was even published, it caught the attention of John August, a screenwriter who had written the indie film *Go*, a hit for Sony in 1999. He managed to persuade Sony to buy the rights to *Big Fish*, for him to adapt. It was a debut novel, so not a huge ask. '[The] book wasn't very plotty', said August. 'I said [to Wallace], "I'm going to have to gather stuff up and make a structure here that isn't really the structure of your book, but know that it's all in the service of some really great truths".' Wallace approved. August gave it a clearer narrative.

The film opens at the wedding of Will and Joséphine Bloom. This should be their day, but Will's dad, Edward, has hogged the spotlight with his far-fetched anecdotes. He always does this, spinning yarns that are patently untrue and making sure attention is always on him. Time moves forward and Will is called home because Edward is dying of cancer. As Will tries to finally find some connection with his father, before it's too late, Edward relays, to anyone who will listen, his version of his life story. It includes werewolves and secret villages, two-headed circus performers and a bank heist, a love that freezes time and the biggest catfish ever seen.

The script attracted the attention of Steven Spielberg, who was attached as director for about a year until he moved on to make *Catch Me If You Can*. It was then that someone suggested Burton.

This wasn't typical material for Burton. All the fantasy stuff was, yes, but the family drama went deeper than he usually ventures. It's sincere, in a way Burton generally isn't. But this script found him at just the right time. It was small(ish), would not be a tentpole film, and most importantly, it would help him. '[The death of my parents] wasn't something that was easy for me to talk about with anybody', Burton said on the film's release, 'but this script was a great way to present that feeling without having to talk about it'.

Big Fish almost requires Burton to direct two different films. One, showing Edward's chosen version of his life, is more traditionally Burton, full of flights of fancy. Edward (played as a boy by Perry Walston, then as a young man by Ewan McGregor) has various outlandish encounters. He meets a witch with a future-seeing eye (Helena Bonham Carter), in a setting that could have been another corner of *Sleepy Hollow*, and ventures through spooky woods with a giant (Matthew McGrory). He seduces his future wife, Sandra (Alison Lohman) with a huge field of daffodils. It's all gorgeous fantasy extravagance – a first and, so far, only collaboration with production designer Dennis Gasner, a favourite of the Coen Brothers – and quintessentially Burton.

The rest was newer territory. The scenes in which Will (Billy Crudup) and his wife, Joséphine (Marion Cotillard), come to visit older Edward (Albert Finney) and Sandra (Jessica Lange), Will's mother, have no gloss or artifice to them. It isn't the stylized domesticity of *Edward Scissorhands*. It's just observing people experiencing real life. It's Burton's filmmaking stripped bare. 'Maybe there was an attempt at some sort of emotional realism that I maybe hadn't quite dealt with before,' Burton said, 'although I always try to make it emotional'. This was his first project with John August, who would become a frequent collaborator, and there was a clear trust between them.

One of the film's most moving and memorable scenes, in which Sandra climbs into a bathtub with her husband and shares a silent hug, knowing there won't be many more, was a fairly late addition. August remembers watching Lange choosing her costumes for the film. 'I noticed that she was picking much sexier outfits than I expected', he said. '"Sandra wants to look good for her husband", she explained. That was kind of genius, but I hadn't given her any scenes that really supported this idea. I wrote the bathtub scene on hotel stationery and showed it to Tim Burton that same evening. That kind of insight only happens [while shooting].'

BELOW: Young Leo Bloom (Ewan McGregor) spots his future wife and time stands still.

The sense of realism is helped by the fact that Burton shot almost everything on location in Alabama. It gives the film a texture that's more humble than Burton's films typically have. 'That spooky forest we creep through,' said McGregor, 'that could quite easily have been built on a soundstage in LA, but it wasn't. It was in a forest in Alabama, and there's something about the flavour of it all that ends up on the screen. . .It helped a lot being down there.'

The final moments of *Big Fish* are the most emotional of any Burton film. As Edward is slipping towards death, Will, who has come to understand that his father's stories are a way of making the mundane more colourful, gives his father the gift of one last grand fable, whispered into his ear. We watch the story he tells. Will races Edward to the river, where everyone special from his life has come to say goodbye, from the werewolf circus-master (Danny DeVito) to the witch to his Sandra. As Will carries his father into the water and lowers him down, Edward turns into a giant catfish and swims off. They both have an ending that helps them make sense of the unknown. It's Burton at his most open-hearted, daring to just feel – and ask his audience to feel – without the protection of fantasy. The film doesn't end with Will's story for his dad. It ends with a funeral. Death is real. It has happened. It's accepted.

After the best part of a decade being buffeted around by the studio system, Burton found making *Big Fish* a refreshing change. 'I haven't had this experience in a long time where a studio wants to do a film that you can't describe in two sentences, isn't a well-known property, doesn't have one star driving it', he said. 'It was a fairly unique experience, and I was appreciative of that.' In multiple ways, it had helped him turn the page on a very difficult time.

LEFT: Will (Billy Crudup) at his wedding, where his father, Edward (Albert Finney), steals his thunder.

CHARLIE AND THE CHOCOLATE FACTORY
2005

As is true for millions of children, reading Roald Dahl was a revelation for the young Tim Burton. *Charlie and the Chocolate Factory* was first published in 1964, when Burton was six years old. When he read it a few years later, it was like someone had finally written a book for him. 'It was one of the first times you had children's literature that was a bit more sophisticated and dealt with darker issues and feelings', he said. It's one of the most successful children's stories of all time, selling more than

20 million copies. A film adaptation, *Willy Wonka & the Chocolate Factory*, directed by Mel Stuart and starring Gene Wilder, was released in 1971. Famously hated by Dahl, and receiving generally tepid reviews, the movie nevertheless built a huge fanbase.

By the mid-90s, Warner Bros was trying to launch a new *Charlie and the Chocolate Factory* film, but with Dahl's estate (Dahl died in 1990) keeping tight control of any new production, it was proving a slow process. Dahl's widow, Felicity, would have final say over all key creatives and insisted on meeting any potentials in person. Gary Ross (*Pleasantville*; 1998, *The Hunger Games*; 2012) was attached for a while, as was Rob Minkoff (*The Lion King*; 1994, *Stuart Little*; 1999). Adam Sandler, Nicolas Cage and Jim Carrey were all mooted Wonkas. It took almost a decade of false starts and resignations before it arrived at Burton's door. 'It was a long fight,' said Felicity Dahl, 'but it pays to wait.'

BELOW: Charlie (Freddie Highmore) and Grandpa Joe (David Kelly) get ready to enter the factory.

Burton already had some history with Dahl. In 1996, he produced a live-action/stop-motion animation hybrid of *James and the Giant Peach*, directed by *Nightmare Before Christmas*' Henry Selick. That film was a box-office flop, but it was well reviewed and Felicity Dahl felt it was one of the few Dahl adaptations to capture his mix of darkness and warmth. She was enthusiastic about Burton directing *Charlie*.

Once onboard, Burton brought on *Big Fish*'s John August to write a new script. Thanks to impending shooting dates, August had just three weeks to complete his first draft. He was unfamiliar with the 1971 version ('It's not like I was raised off the grid by hippie survivalists, but somehow I had never seen it') and purposely avoided it until he had finished his initial pass. When he eventually watched Mel Stuart's film, he said many of its choices 'wouldn't have been my choices'. August's screenplay stays much closer to the book than the 1971 film, with a few additional embellishments.

Charlie Bucket (Freddie Highmore) doesn't have much. He lives in a rickety house with his mother and father (Helena Bonham Carter and Noah Taylor), and four bed-bound grandparents. Their town was once thriving, thanks to the success of Willy Wonka's world-famous chocolate, but following years of attacks from rivals desperate to steal his ingenious ideas, Wonka shuttered his factory. He later quietly reopened it, with no apparent employees and without ever letting outsiders in. When Wonka offers the chance for five children to visit his factory, if they can find the golden tickets hidden in his confectionary, Charlie does all he can to grab one. He winds up on a tour with a gaggle of the worst children you've ever seen: greedy Augustus Gloop (Philip Wiegratz), obnoxious Violet Beauregarde (AnnaSophia Robb), entitled Veruca Salt (Julia Winter), and bratty know-all Mike Teavee (Jordan Fry).

August's script brings back elements from the book, like Wonka's jungle treks and building a chocolate palace for Prince Pondicherry, but he found himself struggling with something that had also hobbled Stuart's film. For all the book's fun and wonder, there's no real arc for either Charlie or Wonka. In the book, Charlie is eventually bequeathed the factory but only because he's not awful like the rest of the children. He earns it by doing nothing. And Wonka is just a guy who wants to give his business away to someone worthy. August thought everyone was missing the real heart of the film. 'Willy Wonka, to me, is the one who's in crisis', he said. 'Why is he inviting people into his factory now? What's going on in his life?' He chose to flip the story round, so 'Charlie Bucket is the antagonist. He's the guy who's causing the change in Willy Wonka'.

It wasn't at all surprising that Burton chose Johnny Depp to be his Wonka. It was quite surprising the direction they headed in. August's script frames Wonka as a man eternally seeking the approval of his dentist father (played, in an entirely invented role, by Christopher Lee). Young Wonka was forbidden from touching chocolate, because it would rot his teeth, but as soon as he tasted it, he was

ABOVE: Wonka's pink dragon boat, filled with 54 animatronic Oompa-Loompas, modelled on Deep Roy.

obsessed. He set his heart on becoming a chocolate mogul, at the cost of his relationship with his dad. The lack of parental affection keeps him locked in a state of arrested development, a weird, lost little boy in the body of a man.

Depp plays him with what he described as 'a combination of the personalities of a game show host and a children's program presenter. His persona comes out of fear and insecurity'. Initially Depp had other ideas. When shooting started, with the chocolate river scene where Wonka begins the tour, Depp was trying an Alfred Hitchcock voice. 'If you look really carefully at that scene [you can see the different performance]', said John August. 'He had to go back and re-voice all that because he was doing a different performance. After about two days, he thought, "You know what, I think I'm going to change how I'm doing all this".'

Many reviews at the time called Depp a mix between Michael Jackson and *Vogue* editor Anna Wintour, thanks to his giant glasses and Prince Valiant haircut. It was the most eccentric Depp had yet been for Burton and he could have been much madder. 'What I was really excited about was a long nose', Depp said at the time. 'I brought it up with Tim, and he was like, "Hang on, hang on. A prosthetic nose? Come on!".'

Charlie and the Chocolate Factory was filmed at Pinewood Studios, on largely practical sets. 'You'll probably never see anything built like this again', said producer Richard Zanuck at the time, and it's true that most directors would have been forced to work against green screen. But not Burton. Everything down to the chocolate river, filled with 927,410 litres (244 995 gallons) of goop (not actual chocolate) was real. He insisted, believing it an essential part of the story. 'I remember from the original book, the feeling of the description and the textures', he said. 'It was important for us to have them be real, and not be stuck in a blue room for six months.' He wanted authenticity everywhere. For the scene in which grasping little Veruca Salt makes one demand too many, insisting she be given one of Wonka's trained squirrels, Burton asked for real animals, so 40 squirrels were taught how to crack nuts on cue.

The film is all big production. Danny Elfman wrote musical numbers that mark the comeuppance of the four horrible children, all in different styles. When Augustus Gloop plops into the chocolate river, it's soundtracked with a Bollywood-style number with Busby

Berkeley choreography. When Violet Beauregarde turns into a giant blueberry, she's rolled away to the strains of a disco-funk jam.

The fact that so much of it was done for real, on real sets, makes a big difference to the final film, which has an appealingly old-fashioned studio picture look. Not everybody loved Depp's take on Wonka, but his high concept fits the film. Freddie Highmore, who had just acted everyone else off the screen in the Depp-starring drama *Finding Neverland* (2004), is the film's secret weapon. Amid all the madness, he's a point of humble, genuine humanity. In this sugar rush of a movie, he keeps it from becoming too sickly.

Charlie and the Chocolate Factory was a huge hit, the biggest of Burton's career so far, with a global total of $476 million. And it wasn't the only film he would be releasing that year.

BELOW: Willy Wonka (Johnny Depp) makes a rare appearance outside his factory.

RIGHT: General Bonesapart (voiced by Deep Roy) leads the dead in song.

CORPSE BRIDE
2005

As if directing one blockbuster movie were not stressful enough, Tim Burton had a side project while making *Charlie and the Chocolate Factory*. In the minimal spare minutes he had available, he was racing from Pinewood Studios in Buckinghamshire to Three Mills Studios in East London to continue making his first animated feature as director, *Corpse Bride*, which had gone into production seven months earlier.

ABOVE: Bonejangles (voiced by Danny Elfman) welcomes Victor (voiced by Johnny Depp) to the underworld.

The concept for *Corpse Bride* had been percolating for over ten years, since it was suggested to Burton by a man called Joe Ranft, a story supervisor on *The Nightmare Before Christmas*. A writer, director and story artist, Ranft was a complete genius of storytelling, with a hand in some of the best animated films of the last 40 years, including *Who Framed Roger Rabbit* (1988), *The Little Mermaid* (1989), *Beauty and the Beast* (1991), *The Lion King* (1994) and *Toy Story* (1995). Tragically, he died in a car crash, a month before *Corpse Bride* was released. The film is dedicated to him.

Ranft and Burton got along well on *Nightmare*. When Ranft happened across a spooky old Jewish folktale, *The Finger,* he thought it would be a match for Burton. *The Finger* tells of a groom-to-be travelling through woods with some friends. They spot what looks like a root poking out of the ground, but on closer inspection it turns out to be the bony finger of a skeleton. As a joke, the man puts a ring on the finger and recites his practised wedding vows. To his horror, the skeleton of a woman rises from the grave and insists the man is now legally her husband. Burton liked it, but it joined the pile of unrealized films at the back of his mind, and sat there gathering dust, waiting to be rediscovered. Warner Bros eventually greenlit it in 2003, then almost immediately asked Burton to direct *Charlie and the Chocolate Factory*. So, he said yes to both.

Burton's version, written by John August (*Charlie and the Chocolate Factory*), Caroline Thompson (*Edward Scissorhands*) and Pamela Pettler, takes the folktale as a loose framework. In a dreary Victorian town, Victor (Johnny Depp), son of the wealthy Van Dort's (Tracey Ullman and Paul Whitehouse), is set to marry Victoria (Emily Watson), daughter of the aristocratic but penniless Everglots (Albert Finney and Joanna Lumley). Victor and Victoria's marriage has been arranged by their parents, but as soon as they meet there's a romantic spark. Having clumsily spoiled their wedding rehearsal, a nervous Victor runs away to the woods and practises his vows, placing a ring on, he thinks, a root. Vows said, an undead woman, Emily (Helena Bonham Carter), reanimates, declares Victor her husband and takes him to the land of the dead to spend their afterlife together. Victor desperately wants to return to Victoria, but he can't do so unless Emily allows it.

The Burton twist is that the land of the living, with its stern morals and stiff formality, is grey and joyless, while the land of the dead is full of colour and celebration. Burton took inspiration from the Mexican Day of the Dead, which he'd always considered an appealing view of the afterlife. 'It's all humour, music and dancing and sort of a celebration of life, in a way, and that always felt more like a positive approach to things', he said. 'So, I always responded to that, more than just this sort of dark, unspoken cloud in the environment I grew up in.'

There was a long struggle with the script and, despite more than a decade between Ranft first raising the idea with Burton and the film going into production, *Corpse Bride* started without a finished script. It's a tricky story to get right. At its heart is a love triangle, but there's no side that deserves to lose. Victor marries Emily by accident, but she thinks he means it. Victoria may only have known Victor for a day, but she still cares about him. And Victor just keeps innocently getting things wrong.

Exactly who wrote what is unclear, though August said his best understanding was 'Caroline wrote a detailed outline, while Pamela wrote the first real script. I was the in-production guy, who did tweaks and fixes'. Rewrites throughout filming are very common on live-action movies, but less frequent on animated films, because the cost of 'reshooting' is so great. A minute of film can take a week to animate. August remembers his job involved a lot of writing on the fly, fixing scenes that were not working but needed to be animated imminently. 'I'd get storyboards from London for scenes that were about to shoot, and would have a day or less to tweak the dialogue before an actor would record the needed lines,' he said, adding 'I felt like a craftsman rather than artist, and that's fine'.

It was, by its nature, a scramble for most people involved. Depp, Bonham Carter and Christopher Lee, who plays a pastor, had to record their vocals when not required on *Charlie and the Chocolate Factory* ('[Johnny] was Willy Wonka by day and Victor by night', joked Burton). It would have been virtually impossible for

ABOVE: Emily Watson voices Victoria, who hopes her fiancé will return to the land of the living.

Burton to be sole director, so he had a co-director, Mike Johnson, who'd worked in the animation departments of *The Nightmare Before Christmas* and *James and the Giant Peach*. 'Tim knew where he wanted the film to go as far as the emotional tone and story points to hit', said Johnson of the partnership. 'My job was to work with the crew on a daily basis and get the footage as close as possible to how I thought he wanted it.'

The animation is far more sophisticated than anything in *The Nightmare Before Christmas*. To create facial expressions on *Nightmare*'s characters, animators would have to repeatedly replace their faces with pre-moulded pieces. On *Corpse Bride*, the puppets all had sophisticated metal skeletons under their silicon skin, full of moveable bits. Animators could stick a screwdriver in a model's ear or under its hair and adjust eyes, mouth or cheekbones. The veil for Emily took weeks of research alone, to try to find ways to animate a flimsy bit of fabric (the answer was fine hidden wires). Some of the film's most breathtaking moments are just Emily walking through a forest in the moonlight.

It may have been a frantic job for almost everyone involved, and is probably regarded as second-tier Burton, but there's a lot that's lovely about *Corpse Bride,* particularly in the musical numbers. The skeleton-sung song, 'Remains of the Day', written and performed by Danny Elfman, feels simultaneously like a tribute to Ray Harryhausen, the classic Disney short 'The Skeleton Dance' and 'Pink Elephants on Parade' from *Dumbo*. And it's impressive that using a colour palette that's almost exclusively grey, the film manages to make the human world look visually ravishing.

After all that effort, there was one big reward for making *Corpse Bride*. It brought Burton his first-ever Oscar nomination, for Best Animated Feature.

TOP RIGHT: It's not wedded bliss for Victor (Johnny Depp) and Emily (Helena Bonham Carter).

RIGHT: Victor's parents, William (voiced by Paul Whitehouse) and Nell Van Dort (voiced by Tracey Ullman).

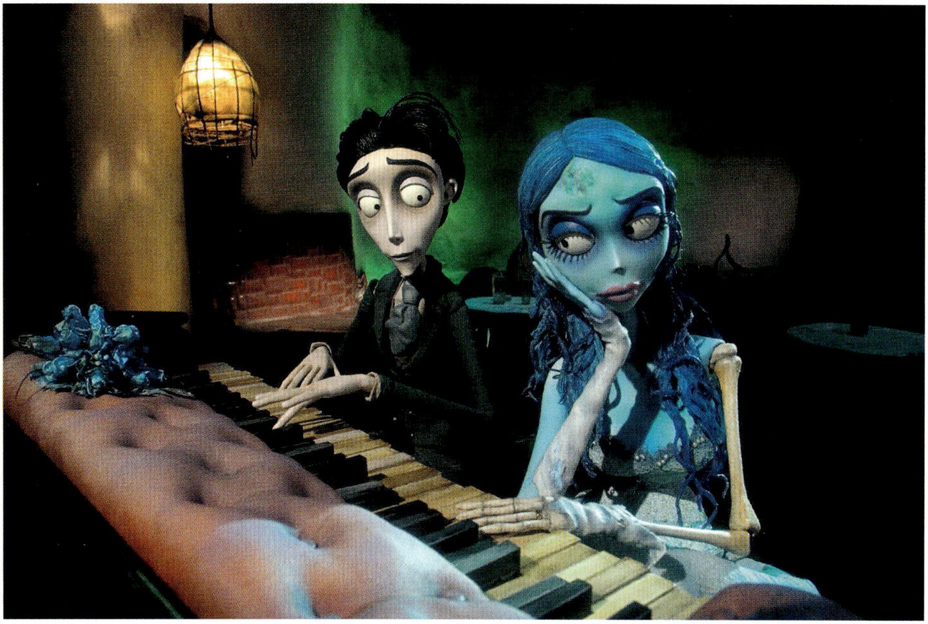

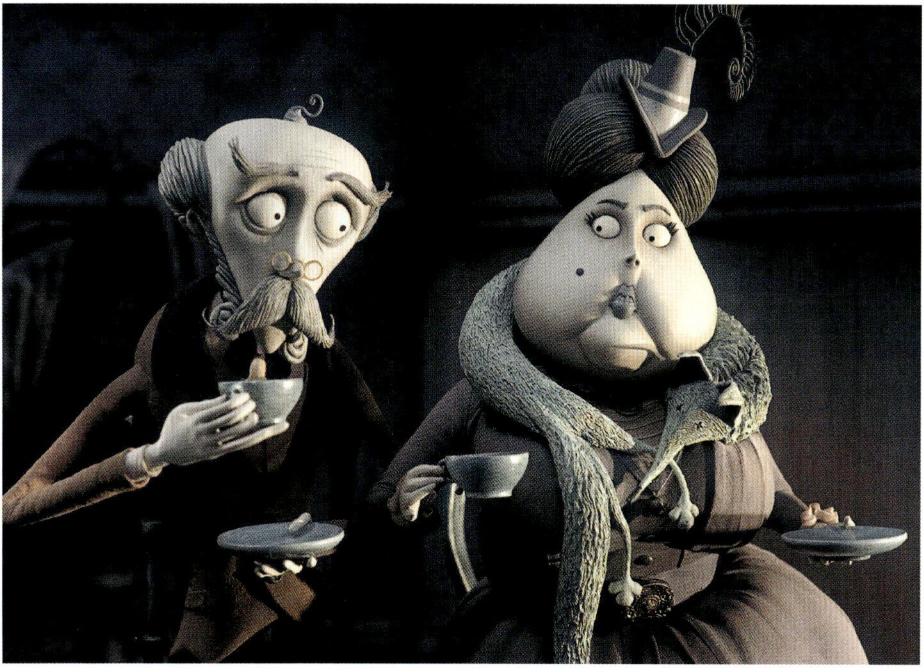

SWEENEY TODD: THE DEMON BARBER OF FLEET STREET
2007

The first time Tim Burton came to England, as a college student from sunny Burbank, California, he thought, 'I'm home! There's texture! There's weather! There's seasons!' A kid who grew up fantasizing about the foggy streets of Universal monster movies and Hammer Horror had found his place, full of stout old buildings, drizzle and an abundance of grey. It was on that first trip, in 1980, that Burton saw something that would become a lifelong obsession.

Burton doesn't like musicals, as a rule, but when he went to a production of Stephen Sondheim's *Sweeney Todd: The Demon Barber of Fleet Street* at London's National Theatre, he was hooked. So hooked that, as he remembers, he went about 12 times.

'I didn't know who Stephen Sondheim was', he said. 'I think I just saw the poster and wandered into the theatre and it blew me away. I went three nights in a row.' The show could have been made for Burton. Based on a 19th-century penny dreadful story, it tells of Benjamin Barker, a London barber who was exiled to Australia on false charges by a judge who wanted to steal Barker's wife for his own. Years later, he returns to London with a new name, Sweeney Todd, and a lust for revenge. He opens a barber shop where he slices the throats of any man who upsets him and gives their bodies to his neighbour, Mrs Lovett, a pitiful pie shop owner who is grateful for the free meat and the attention of Sweeney. With lots of blood and danger, and a set full of cinematic drama, the show burrowed into Burton's mind and brooded there. 'The emotion was so strong. And the humour and the graphicness of it', he said.

With Burton's career taking off, sometime around the release of *Beetlejuice* in 1988, he approached Sondheim about the possibility of turning *Sweeney Todd* into a movie. By this time, the show had grown into something of a minor classic, with Tonys and Oliviers and an impending Broadway revival. Sondheim had little reason to trust this upstart director, but he said yes, why not? But other things got in the way – like *Batman* – and *Sweeney* would have to wait a while longer.

Burton, as always, had drawn ideas for how his *Sweeney* might look. He rarely throws his drawings away, and, in 2005, he found a *Sweeney* sketch in a box. To him, it looked just like Johnny Depp and Helena Bonham Carter. It got his mind ticking. He went back to Stephen Sondheim. The answer was still yes.

When he began developing *Sweeney Todd*, Burton had no actual idea if either Depp or Bonham Carter could sing. He knew Bonham Carter wanted to play Mrs Lovett, because they lived together and shared a mutual love for the musical. They had talked about it on one of their first dates. Bonham Carter had been listening to the soundtrack since she was a child. As soon as Burton decided it

RIGHT: Mrs Lovett (Helena Bonham Carter) is a woman with more secrets than she can handle.

was his next project, she began taking singing lessons to see if she could build the vocal chops for the role. Depp agreed to play Sweeney before anyone, himself included, had confirmed he could sing. 'Sets were being constructed, wardrobe was being made', remembered the late producer Richard Zanuck. 'We were literally spending millions of dollars on the picture and not one person on Earth had heard Johnny sing.'

Sondheim's songs are famously hard to perform. His melodies dart in unexpected directions and he rarely leaves the singer anywhere to breathe. *Sweeney Todd* isn't a musical for beginners. 'When Tim asked if I'd be into it,' recalled Depp, 'he said, "Do you think you can sing?" And I said, "Honestly, I don't know."' Thankfully, after a few sessions with music producer Bruce Witkin, a former bandmate of Depp's, it was decided that, yes, he would be able to do it.

Sweeney Todd isn't the first musical film Burton had made. *The Nightmare Before Christmas, Corpse Bride* and *Charlie and the Chocolate Factory* all have musical numbers, but they're not full-on musicals. *Sweeney Todd* is, if not entirely sung-through,

The World of Stainboy

In 1997, Burton published *The Melancholy Death of Oyster Boy & Other Stories*, a book of illustrated tales about oddball children who often come to unpleasant ends. The Oyster Boy of the title is eaten by his own father.

In 2000, one of those characters, a bog-eyed superhero called Stainboy, became the star of a series of animated shorts, in which he works for the Burbank police and is sent on missions to kill other freaky children. All directed by Burton, they were released online under the banner *The World of Stainboy*. They're among the darkest things he's ever made. One episode ends with a dog taking a bite out of an expired Toxic Boy and keeling over, dead. Not suitable for kids.

ABOVE: Sacha Baron Cohen plays Adolfo Pirelli, Benjamin Barker's former apprentice.

very close to it. Directing it required a higher level of discipline than almost any of Burton's previous films. You can't really improvise a lyric in a musical (especially as all the vocals were recorded before filming) or insert a new scene on a whim. Burton, who was so used to films being retooled throughout production, would have to be absolutely rigorous here.

That isn't to say that he didn't cut himself some slack. The movie slices a good hour out of the stage musical. Anything too 'theatrical' is gone, like the opening number, 'Attend the Tale of Sweeney Todd', that sets up the story. And the romantic subplot of Sweeney's young friend Anthony (Jamie Campbell Bower) and his secret daughter, Johanna (Jayne Wisener) is severely truncated, so it becomes a film almost entirely focused on Sweeney Todd and Mrs Lovett.

Burton makes Todd even more dour than in the stage musical (Burton and Depp would routinely cut down Todd's lines during shooting) and contrasts him with the comic, eternally pathetically hopeful Mrs Lovett. Neither Depp nor Bonham Carter are especially strong singers, but they're both superb actors, so the odd thin note hardly matters. Burton had very different direction for his leads. Depp's performance was inspired by the likes of Peter Lorre, Boris Karloff and Lon Chaney, actors who expressed a lot while saying little. For Bonham Carter, it was about doing the least possible. She was instructed not to use her hands and to try not to move her eyebrows. She remembers Burton told her, 'Because you're singing

BELOW: Judge Turpin (Alan Rickman), the man who drove Benjamin Barker to become Sweeney Todd.

and you're already in a big environment. . .you've got to counteract that with a very restrained performance'.

Where Burton absolutely didn't hold back is in the film's gore. A parade of British character actors – Sasha Baron Cohen as a flamboyant fake Italian barber who tries to blackmail Todd; Alan Rickman as the dastardly judge who stole Todd's wife; and Timothy Spall as the judge's oleaginous assistant – all meet their ends in floods of blood. 'He had a very clear plan that he wanted to lift that up into a surreal, almost *Kill Bill* kind of stylization', said Zanuck. Gallons of bright red liquid latex were sloshed around the set.

For all its murder and depression, there's something quite joyful about *Sweeney Todd*. You can sense Burton's glee at playing in the world. He had a 'horror movie London' built at Pinewood Studios, which he could treat like a playground. The Grand Guignol carnage of the story and surrealism of the musical structure suit him. He directs and edits well to the rhythms of each number and lets his imagination fly in ways that wouldn't be possible on stage. *By the Sea*, Mrs Lovett's daydream about a life with Sweeney, becomes a series of fantasy sequences, transporting the pair from their monochrome lives to a cavalcade of colourful adventures.

Burton has never been shy about admitting when he hasn't had the best experience making his films. On *Sweeney Todd,* it seemed he genuinely had a delightful time in his world of rat-infested streets and violent murder. 'I've got to say,' he confessed, 'I enjoyed making this one more than many others.'

'What sorcery is this?'

BRAND
BURTON

LEFT: Alice (Mia Wasikowska) surveys the dubious charms of the ravaged Underland.

ALICE IN WONDERLAND
2010

Tim Burton has always expressed a deep appreciation for craftsmanship. When his movies require animated elements, he usually wants to realize them using stop-motion, the most labour-intensive option. On *Charlie and the Chocolate Factory,* when most directors would have created the factory using green screen, he insisted on practical sets. So why did one of modern cinema's biggest proponents of doing things the old way find himself making a movie that had no sets whatsoever? To fully understand why Burton made Disney's mega-budget *Alice in Wonderland,* you have to consider what was happening in the world of cinema at the time.

Through the 2000s, 3D was becoming a huge trend in cinema. Technology was progressing swiftly, giving directors the ability to create movies that could almost literally pull the viewer into a new world. Prestige directors were pushing its boundaries. In 2009, James Cameron's *Avatar* was released. With production and marketing costs of around $400 million, it was widely assumed it would never turn a profit. It became the biggest film of all time, with an initial box-office run of $2.7 billion. That was, in large part, thanks to its use of cutting-edge 3D.

Every studio wanted part of the 3D pie. When Burton was offered *Alice in Wonderland,* in 2007, he saw the chance for two things: 1) to bring his vision to a story many have attempted but few have nailed, and 2) to experiment with a shiny new toy. 'Disney came to me with the idea of doing *Alice in Wonderland* in 3-D, and that seemed intriguing,' he said. 'The movie versions I'd seen, to me, were always just, like, a little brat wandering around a bunch of weirdos.'

Despite the title, Burton's *Alice in Wonderland* isn't a remake of the 1951 Disney animation, nor really a reinterpretation of Lewis Caroll's book. It's sort of a sequel to the Disney film, though Burton never referred to it as such. It opens with a teenage Alice (Mia Wasikowska) at a grand country gathering, which she discovers is intended to be her engagement party, to a man she doesn't like and hasn't agreed to marry. When Alice spots a white rabbit and pursues it, she trips and falls down a hole, which takes her to Underland, a ravaged version of what was once Wonderland. Underland is full of fantastical creatures, but it's far from wondrous. Ruled over by the tyrannical Red Queen (Helena Bonham Carter), it's a dark and dangerous place where anyone who even slightly upsets the monarch risks having their head chopped off. When Alice comes across the Hatter (Johnny Depp), she learns that she's prophesied to free Underland by slaying the monstrous Jabberwocky.

Almost none of this is in either Carroll's *Alice in Wonderland,* nor its sequel, *Through the Looking Glass*. The Jabberwocky, a great dragon-like creature, features in a poem in *Through the Looking Glass*, but Alice never encounters it, let alone slays it. The whole plot was the invention of Linda Woolverton, best known for writing Disney's *Beauty and the Beast* (1991). '[The 'Jabberwocky'] poem was a launching pad for me, really', said Woolverton.

ABOVE: The Red Queen (Helena Bonham Carter) vows to find the villain that ate her jam tarts.

'"Jabberwocky" actually influenced me more than the two books.' As in the poem, it's a tale full of violence and fear.

Burton liked that this Alice isn't, as he puts it, a 'brat', standing up to everyone she meets. She's confused about her place in the world and realizes the only way to have the life she wants is to take control of it. By the end, she has slain the Jabberwocky in Underland and at home she has declined her suitor and embarked on her own career as an adventurer. 'It's a simple internal story about somebody finding their own strength', said Burton. 'She's been battered around by real life, has never quite fitted in. . .' The classic Burton theme.

Ninety per cent of *Alice* – pretty much everything but the party scenes – was shot against green screen, across 40 days on an LA

soundstage. Working with green screen wasn't new to Burton. Though you may not spot it, thanks to the superb digital effects, a good number of *Sweeney Todd*'s outdoor sequences were shot against green screen, with grubby London drawn in later. *Alice* was of an altogether different order. Production designer Robert Stromberg, who'd worked on *Avatar*, designed the digital 'sets' ahead of shooting, so the cast could look at images of what was meant to be there; otherwise they had to imagine everything. The actors would perform in a sea of green onto which Underland would

ABOVE: The Mad Hatter (Johnny Depp), minus hat, brandishes the Jabberwocky-slaying vorpal sword.

later be grafted. It's a huge test of an actor's skill. 'I like an obstacle – I don't mind having to spew dialogue while having to step over dolly track while some guy is holding a card and I'm talking to a piece of tape,' said Depp, 'but the green beats you up. You're kind of befuddled at the end of the day.'

The benefit of green screen is that Burton could choose what every aspect of Underland, down to the smallest leaf, looks like. Technically, it's very impressive. When Alice first plops into Underland, she's surrounded by a forest of oversized, jewel-coloured flowers, and greeted by, among others, a talking dodo (Michael Gough), the White Rabbit (Michael Sheen) and two eerie dough-faced twins, Tweedledum and Tweedledee (both Matt Lucas). All are digital creations. It's a shame that Burton doesn't really get to give his full vision of *Wonderland*, other than in a final act flashback when Alice remembers her first visit. Underland is like Wonderland after a nuclear attack, all rubble and dry scrub. It might have been nice to see what Burton could make of the magical world in its pomp. For all the digital wizardry, there's nothing in the film to match the tactile nature of the spooky forest in *Big Fish* or the chocolate river in *Charlie and the Chocolate Factory.* A lot of the Burton charm is lost in the slickness of special effects.

The gonzo setting lets the actors go wild with their performances. Helena Bonham Carter, in her sixth collaboration with Burton, is a hoot as the Red Queen, with a bulbous head and lisping bellow. She takes things over the top and then just keeps going. Depp's performance was divisive. Burton has always allowed his most frequent star to colour outside the lines, but Depp may have lost control of his crayons on this one. His Mad Hatter leans more towards the certifiable than the endearingly kooky. With his yellow eyes, pale face and wild orange hair, he looks like the unholy offspring of Ronald McDonald and Pennywise from *It* (2017). His voice ranges through simpering English to 'hoots mon' Scottish with the odd possessed growl. It's certainly a lot, whether it's too much will depend on the viewer.

Reaction to *Alice* was mixed. *The Hollywood Reporter* called it 'a fantastical romp' and many reviews praised its design, but others, like *The New York Observer*, were unimpressed, suggesting 'it might be time for Tim Burton and Johnny Depp to start thinking about seeing other people'. *Alice* is, though, by a very long way, Burton's biggest hit. It made over a billion dollars, almost double the box office of his second biggest success, *Charlie and the Chocolate Factory*. As an experiment for Burton, it was a financially very lucrative one. As a test of whether he would like to work in this way again, the result was less convincing. 'We were designing as we went along', he said of the process. 'Honestly, since it was all done like puzzle pieces, I didn't even see the movie until it was done. . .It was the most backwards, disturbing process I've ever been through.' He didn't return for its sequel.

TOP RIGHT: The White Rabbit is voiced by Welsh actor Michael Sheen.

RIGHT: Twins Tweedledum and Tweedledee are both played by Matt Lucas, with help from double Ethan Cohn.

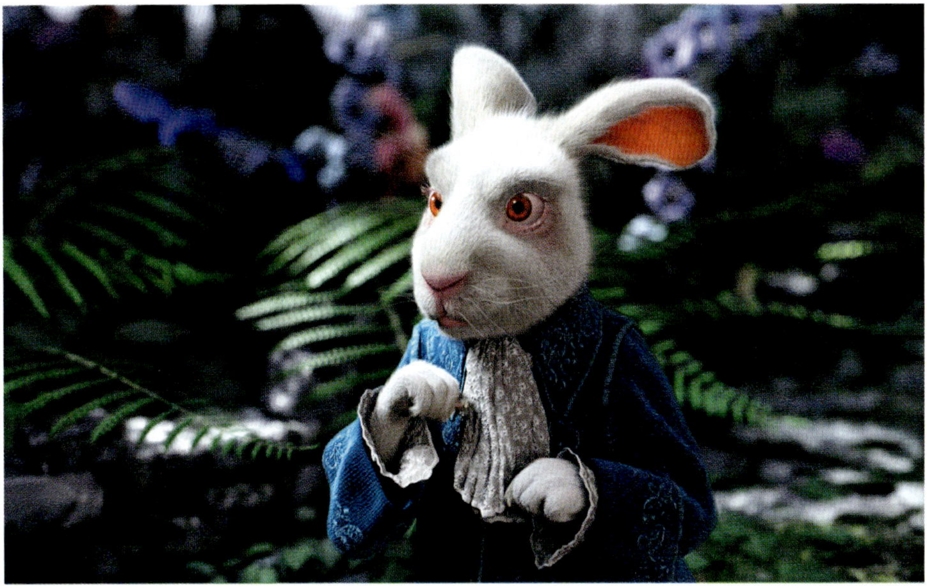

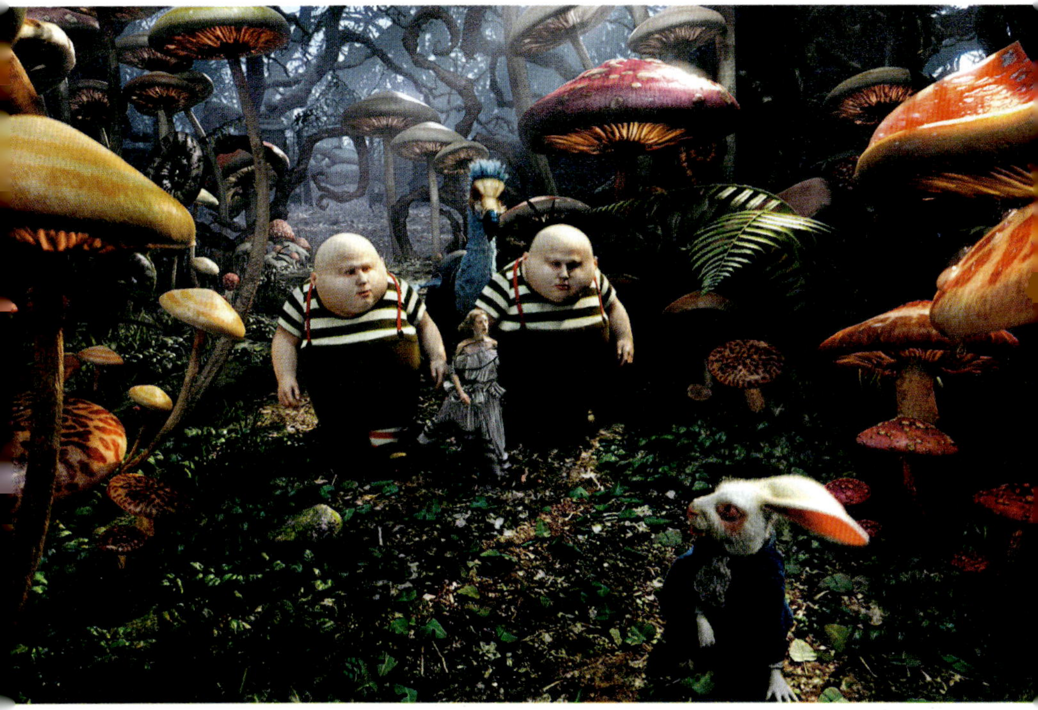

DARK
SHADOWS
2012

Michelle Pfeiffer isn't in the habit of calling directors to ask if she can be in their movies. She has only done it a few times in her entire career. But when she heard that Tim Burton might be adapting one of her favourite TV shows, she picked up the phone and asked if there might be something in it for her. *Dark Shadows*

isn't a particularly memorable part of the Tim Burton canon, but it's notable for reuniting Burton with one of his greatest leading actors, for the first time since *Batman Returns* in 1992.

Dark Shadows is a surprising series for anyone to feel especially passionate about. Aired in the United States from 1966–71, it's a high-camp, goth soap-opera about the Collins family, whose lives are full of spooky things like vampires, werewolves and curses. Made with a clearly ungenerous budget, it was famed for its endearingly cheap effects, like rubber bats on strings bobbing across the screen. It may not be obvious what Pfeiffer saw in it, but its mix of kitsch and goth places it firmly in the Burton wheelhouse.

'It was sort of like a weird dream', is Burton's best description of the show's appeal, which he remembers watching after school in Burbank. Equally smitten with it was Johnny Depp, who, Burton said, had wanted to act in *Dark Shadows* 'ever since he was a little boy'. It was Depp who asked Burton to make the film. Seth Grahame-Smith, who wrote the Burton-produced *Abraham Lincoln: Vampire Hunter* (2012), was brought in to try to wrangle the very old-fashioned, extremely tacky property into a big-budget Hollywood blockbuster.

The story begins in 1760, with Barnabas Collins (Depp), handsome playboy son of the well-to-do Collins family. Barnabas incurs the wrath of Angelique (Eva Green), his maid, who also happens to be a witch, after he rejects her. Angelique murders Barnabas's parents, curses him to become a vampire, and enchants his fianceé Josette (Bella Heathcote), causing her to leap from a cliff to her death. The townspeople, terrified by Barnabas's blood-sucking transformation, trap him in a coffin and bury him.

In 1972, Victoria (also Heathcote), a young woman with a startling resemblance to Josette, comes to Collinwood Manor looking for work. There she finds the family down on its luck, with

ABOVE: Helena Bonham Carter plays the ill-fated alcoholic psychiatrist Dr Julia Hoffman.

matriarch Elizabeth (Pfeiffer) heading a meagre, miserable brood of her daughter, Carolyn (Chloë Grace Moretz); wayward brother Roger (Jonny Lee Miller); Roger's unhappy son, David (Gully McGrath); and David's alcoholic psychiatrist (Helena Bonham Carter). They're all scraping out an impoverished existence thanks to their family business being wiped out by a competitor. . .a still very much young and vigorous Angelique, who has dedicated centuries to getting revenge on Barnabas. When Barnabas is accidentally dug up, Angelique gets another shot at vengeance.

It's a tangled old plot for a bit of light, soap-opera fun and presents a tricky tone for Burton to balance. On set, Burton wanted to pay homage to the cheesiness of the original show, without going the full rubber bat. 'How *Dark Shadows* am I today?' Pfeiffer would ask when she arrived on set (she would watch DVDs of the show in make-up every morning, to get herself in the mood). But

ABOVE: Eva Green as centuries-old witch Angelique Bouchard, who has never lost her passion for Barnabas.

the tone ultimately tripped Burton up. 'I always knew that it was dangerous territory', he said several years after the film's release, when asked why it had not worked. '[The show] had the weirdest tone. I always found the show, even though it was deadly serious, quite comedic.' That's where *Dark Shadows* falls down. At times it's trying to be genuinely scary, as Barnabas rips apart construction workers or unsuspecting hippies. Then, in the next scene, Barnabas will be hammily sinking his fangs into the scenery. It's hard for the audience to know how to respond. Depp gives it plenty, turning in the sort of performance with which Ed Wood might be thrilled, but all the vamping in the world can't disguise a lack of coherent plot.

It's disappointing that it doesn't work, because it certainly shows potential. Visually, it's splendid, with grand production design by Rick Heinrichs, who built an entire harbour-side town, complete

ABOVE: Victoria Winters (Bella Heathcote) bears an eerie resemblance to Barnabas' lost love, Josette.

with movie theatre and lapping sea. And Bruno Delbonell's cinematography manages a look that's Hammer Horror-meets-70s-disco (Delbonell would go on to work with Burton again on *Big Eyes* and *Miss Peregrine's Home for Peculiar Children*). On all the design fronts, it's one of Burton's more sumptuous films. It's just a shame it isn't in service of a better story.

And after all that time apart, it's a rather flat reunion with Pfeiffer. Looking very imperious, with magnificently huge hair, she gets little to do beyond casting withering looks from the top of Collinwood Manor's sweeping staircase.

Thankfully, there was a much better horror-comedy just around the corner, wagging its friendly little tail. And this one would bring another reunion with one of Burton's best collaborators, from even earlier in his career.

FRANKENWEENIE
2012

In 2005, while doing double directing duty on *Charlie and the Chocolate Factory* and *Corpse Bride*, Tim Burton made himself a promise. He would, he vowed, never do this again. Making two films at once was simply too much for one man. Yet somehow, in 2011, he found himself repeating the experience almost identically, right down to shooting at the same facilities. When not at Pinewood Studios making *Dark Shadows*, Burton was at Three Mills Studios in East London, resurrecting a character he had already killed once, back in 1984.

Frankenweenie was the short film that ignited his filmmaking career, telling the story of a boy who brings his beloved dead dog back to life. Turning it into a feature wasn't Burton's idea. Producer Don Hahn (*The Lion King*; 1994) approached Burton while he was working on *Charlie and the Chocolate Factory*. 'I was around at [Disney] when Tim did the original short, back in the early 80s,' said Hahn. 'So I went back to Tim. . .and said, you have this great story . . .There's got to be more to it, there has to be more of a plot here, because it's inspired by *Frankenstein*.' Hahn was correct. Burton

ABOVE: Sparky the dog's look was inspired by the Burton-produced 1987 cartoon series *Family Dog*.

knew just how to make it bigger. 'I've had ideas for a long time about how to expand it', he said.

The expanded *Frankenweenie* is what you might get if you tipped Burton upside down and shook out the contents of his brain. The heart of the story is just as it is in the 1984 short, but all the extra elements are drawn either from Burton's own life or his lifelong passions. 'Everything in it is based on somebody I knew or a composite of some people', said Burton. 'All the places and emotions and kid politics are very real to me. It was a way to apply every memory and every feeling you had and put it in one place.'

For a start, it's made using stop-motion animation, one of Burton's oldest loves, although that was also a case of practicality, given the limited range of canine actors. 'We wanted real dog emotions, and it's a little easier to try to get that in animation', Burton said. The town of New Holland is based on Burbank, Burton's hometown ('Tim wanted the town to be boring', said production designer Rick Heinrichs). Young Victor Frankenstein (voiced by Charlie Tahan) attends a school where most of the other pupils are inspired by characters from horror. And his science teacher bears a striking resemblance to Burton's childhood hero, Vincent Price.

After Victor's pet, Sparky, is hit by a car, and Victor brings him back to life, his secret is discovered by a ghoulish classmate Edgar Gore (Atticus Shaffer), who is clearly based on the hunchbacked horror perennial Igor. Edgar insists on being shown how Victor raised the dead, then blabs to the rest of the class: Toshiaki (James Hiroyuki Liao), who, with his ever-present video camera, seems to be a wink to the Japanese horror directors Burton worshipped; Nassor (Martin Short), who looks and sounds just like *Frankenstein* actor Boris Karloff; Weird Girl (Catherine O'Hara), near identical to Staring Girl from Burton's *The Melancholy Death of Oyster Boy*; and Bob (Robert Capron), who would appear to be just a large boy.

With the class science fair looming, all the children compete to create their own undead pet, and in the final act all those unfortunate experiments wreak havoc on the town, in homage to many kinds of horror. A tiny, mummified hamster is like a mini Universal monster; a turtle becomes a *kaiju*, like Godzilla or Gamera; a troupe of sea monkeys are part *Creature From The Black Lagoon* part *Critters*; and a cat-bat mutant looks like it has flown straight out of a Ray Harryhausen sequence. This is the first stop-motion animation Burton directed on his own (Mike Johnson co-directed *Corpse Bride*) and it's quintessentially him.

Among the voice cast, there are several old Burton favourites. Catherine O'Hara, who played Lydia Deetz in *Beetlejuice* and voiced Sally in *The Nightmare Before Christmas*, does triple duty as Victor's mother, a gym teacher and Weird Girl. As does Martin Short (*Mars Attacks!*), who takes on Victor's father, grouchy neighbour Mr Burgermeister, and Nassor. The most heartwarming return, though, is that of Winona Ryder, working with Burton for the first time since *Edward Scissorhands*. She voices one of Victor's few friends, Elsa Van Helsing, a tribute to both *Bride of Frankenstein* actor Elsa Lanchester and Dracula foe Van Helsing. 'Elsa is sort of a younger Lydia [from *Beetlejuice*], in a way', said Ryder. 'I drew on that and on my feelings for Tim, for Elsa's feelings for Victor.'

That encapsulates what a lovely, warm film *Frankenweenie* is. It's Burton returning to his roots in multiple ways. It even has the look of old stop-motion, with the textures a little rough in places and the movement a smidge jerky. That was a deliberate choice. 'On *Corpse Bride*, our puppets were so sophisticated that people thought they were [animated] in the computer', said Burton. 'It sort of undermined the beauty of the stop-motion technique. So, with *Frankenweenie*, we have a smaller budget and decided that the puppets are going to have to be a bit cruder.' It completely works, giving the film a much more touched-by-human-hands feel.

In an era when a lot of Burton's films seemed more like studio product than the impassioned creations that marked his early career, *Frankenweenie* is a welcome reminder of the old Burton. Having sworn he would never again direct two films simultaneously, Burton had no regrets. 'Honestly, I enjoyed it this time!' he said. However, when asked if he might consider doing the double again, he answered, 'Well, I don't know about that. . .'

RIGHT: Edgar Gore (voiced by Atticus Shaffer), Victor's creepy classmate, inspired by horror hunchback Igor.

'I'm no expert, but I think you have bigger problems'

THE LOST YEARS

BIG EYES
2014

Although she couldn't have known it at the time, Tim Burton's favourite high-school art teacher, Mrs Adams, was the one who set him on his path to becoming an animator. A lot of teachers would discourage the teenage Burton's near-constant doodling and try to get him to focus on his assigned work, but Mrs Adams did all she could to feed his imagination. She loved to watch him unleash the contents of his mind onto paper. She marvelled as he scribbled away, long after the rest of the class had put down their pens. She showed him how to use a camera to make stop-motion films. 'You keep it up and don't you ever stop', she would tell him.

Mrs Adams was the first person to make the young Burton believe that his weird little drawings were worth something, and that he should never change who he is or try to do things like other people. About 40 years later, Burton was sent a script that brought back the feelings Mrs Adams had instilled in him. *Big Eyes* is a movie about finding belief in yourself and, with its complete absence of fantasy, it's Burton testing himself as a storyteller.

ABOVE: Amy Adams originally turned down the role of Margaret, before reconsidering.

Based on a true story, *Big Eyes* follows the life of Margaret Keane, a woman who had to battle her own husband in court just for the right to paint. The film begins in 1958, with the recently divorced Margaret Ulbrich arriving in San Francisco with her daughter, Jane. Margaret loves painting and hopes to make a living from her work, but finds little success. Her works are all of children with huge, sad eyes. Kitsch, but distinctive, they're not for everybody.

Margaret is no great self-publicist and only sells the occasional piece in street markets. Then she meets Walter Keane. Walter is a fellow painter – or at least claims to be – but more than that he's an exceptional marketeer. He can sell almost anything to anyone. Walter romances Margaret and they quickly marry. While trying to sell his own paintings, without success, he flogs a few of Margaret's. They become more and more popular and, jealous of Margaret's attention, Walter pretends her work is his own. He's the one who's good at being a celebrity, so, he thinks, it makes more sense for him to be the 'face' of the work.

Walter becomes one of the most successful 'artists' in the country, making millions of dollars from Margaret's work, as she paints in anonymity behind closed doors. Eventually, Walter's behaviour becomes so monstrous that Margaret leaves him and tries to reclaim her work. As happened in real life, the bitter case goes to court, where a judge decides the only reliable way to prove who really created the big-eyed children is to have Margaret and Walter paint live in front of him.

The script, written by the *Ed Wood* team of Scott Alexander and Larry Karaszewski, appealed to Burton because it's centred on a woman who creates art that she loves, and that many other people love, but that's reviled by most critics. For all the commercial success of the work, the art establishment always looked down on Keane. John Canaday of *The New York Times* (waspishly depicted in the film by Terence Stamp) once described Keane's paintings as 'the very definition of tasteless hack work'. Burton has been dismissed by critics throughout his career, since *Pee-wee's Big Adventure*. He knows what it is to forge your own unappreciated path. 'Ed Wood thought *Plan 9* was probably *Star Wars* and the Keanes thought they were making the *Mona Lisa*', he said. 'I understand that passion.'

After a long run of enormous budget films, *Big Eyes* was Burton's return to filmmaking in an indie style. It cost just $10 million, less than a tenth of the budget for *Dark Shadows*. It has minimal special effects and relatively muted production design (by Rick Heinrichs and Shane Vieau, who were BAFTA nominated). 'Given all the other stuff I'd done, it was nice to keep it simple and let the strangeness of the story be the thing', said Burton.

It's the first film since Burton's earliest days to feature a cast entirely new to him. Amy Adams plays Margaret, a role she originally turned down. 'When I first read the script, I was interested in exploring more confident women', she said. 'But then re-reading it, having had my daughter, having grown up a little bit, having moved away from people's opinions about my work, I was like: You

know what? I really appreciate the complexities of her character.' Oscar-winner Christoph Waltz plays Walter. Of assembling an entirely new troupe, Burton joked, 'Because I'm not a social person, it's a great way to meet people'.

BELOW: Walter (Christoph Waltz) hides the terrible truth that he has no real artistic talent.

Perhaps because it's so modest in comparison to the rest of his films, *Big Eyes* has become a bit of a forgotten moment in Burton's filmography, but it's one of the better films of his latter-stage career. If tonally it has a few wobbles, it's some of Burton's best work with actors. Adams plays Margaret as delicate but determined, a sharp contrast to the bullish Waltz as Walter. This is best displayed in the pivotal court scene, in which Margaret quietly and deliberately gets on with her painting, while Walter dramatically fakes an arm injury and insists he couldn't possibly paint today.

Big Eyes earned respectable reviews and a Golden Globe win for Adams, in Best Actress in a Comedy or Musical (dubious categorization, given the film isn't a comedy by any traditional definition, but a win is a win). It wasn't a box-office success – with $29 million worldwide, it's the second-lowest grossing Burton film after *Ed Wood* – but it seems like a necessary film for the director. After a run of high-concept, stressful projects, this was Burton breathing a big sigh.

MISS PEREGRINE'S HOME FOR PECULIAR CHILDREN
2016

LEFT: Miss Peregrine (Eva Green) introduces Jake (Asa Butterfield) to her children.

Almost as soon as 20th Century Fox secured the rights for *Miss Peregrine's Home for Peculiar Children,* in 2011, Burton was in the frame to direct. He was the obvious choice to adapt Ransom Riggs's best-selling novel, about a group of children whose bizarre powers make them prey for a horde of child-eating monsters.

Riggs, a former blogger and maker of short films, wrote his hit novel almost by accident. Since childhood, he had been collecting strange antique photographs. When he was a pre-teen, his grandmother would drag him around secondhand shops. On one visit, he spotted a black-and-white picture of a girl who looked like

ABOVE: The peculiar children are based on characters created by Ransom Riggs.

someone he had a crush on, so he bought it. Later, when he read the back of the photo and saw the girl had died at the age of 15, he thought, 'Wow, I've been living with a ghost.' Over the years, he collected more photos, always wondering about the lives of the haunted-looking people, often children, in the faded pictures. Eventually, he went to a publisher with the idea of gathering the photos into a book, but they suggested instead using the pictures as the starting point for a novel. And that's how *Miss Peregrine's Home for Peculiar Children* shivered into life.

At the book's heart is Jacob, whose grandfather keeps telling him stories of growing up in a home run by Miss Peregrine, a woman who took in children with remarkable abilities that ranged from invisibility to super strength to the power to bring back the dead.

These children were hunted by monsters, the wights, who wanted to feed on their power. When Jacob's grandfather dies, seemingly killed by something supernatural, Jacob discovers his tales were not invented. He stumbles across the home, which is stuck in a time loop, and has to help the children fend off the dreaded wights.

Burton was keen before seeing a script. The weird children, of course, are pure Burton, but he also loved the fact that the story took place in a time loop. Miss Peregrine's home was destroyed in 1940 by German bombs. Thanks to a magical device, she managed to stop time just before the bombs hit and now she and the children relive the same day over and over, until such time as they can work out how to escape. And then there's Jacob – Jake in the film – another boy who is considered a weirdo by everyone around him, but discovers being weird is better than being normal. It's all textbook Burton stuff.

This makes it that much odder that *Miss Peregrine* never quite comes together, but has the feel of someone *trying* to make a movie in the style of Tim Burton, and not getting it right. Perhaps it's that the plot is complicated, leaving little room to have fun with the concept. Jane Goldman's (*X-Men: First Class*; 2011) script has to set up Jake's life, get him back in time to Miss Peregrine's home, introduce all the children, explain the time loop, explain Miss Peregrine and the other ymbrynes (child-protectors who can turn into birds), explain the wights, and then bring it all together in an action-packed showdown. Is it any wonder things are muddled?

The film is at its most fun when it steps away from the central narrative. A dinner scene where the children reveal their peculiarities has some of the old Burton magic. A quiet boy unleashes the bees that live inside him. A sweet little girl lifts her blond ringlets to feed the razor-toothed mouth in the back of her head. And a scene where Jake (Asa Butterworth) and Emma (Ella Purnell), a girl who can control air, have a chaste afternoon on a shipwreck at the bottom of the sea is full of whimsy. But the story wanders away from Burton, leading to a confused final act, in which the head wight (Samuel L Jackson) and a bunch of CG monsters try to eat the children. By that point, the film seems to have lost Burton's interest.

If there's something noteworthy in *Miss Peregrine*'s finale, it's that this is only the second Burton film to feature a cameo appearance by the director. In *Pee-wee's Big Adventure* he popped up very briefly as a street thug who threatens Pee-wee. Here, you can catch him for a couple of frames in the scene where passengers on fairground rides are caught in the children's battle with the wights. On one of those rides you will see Burton getting pelted with a skeleton. It was, he says, not really his choice to be on screen. 'It was at the end [of shooting]', he said. 'We had no money. We had no crew. We had no [filming] permits. So just a few of us snuck onto a couple of rides. We got kicked off the pier a few times.' But they got the shot.

Few people would consider *Miss Peregrine* the worst film of Burton's, but it's a discordant note. His heart just doesn't seem in it. In 2024, Burton stated that in recent years he'd got a little bit disillusioned with the movie industry'. While he doesn't

ABOVE: Jake (Asa Butterfield) anchors Emma (Ella Purnell) who has the power to manipulate air.

mention the film expressly, you have to wonder if *Miss Peregrine* is where that disillusionment began. His enthusiasm was certainly waning when he got into the thick of his next film. That was an experience so bad, he thought it might be his last.

RIGHT: Dumbo soars above
the crowd at the Medici
Brothers' Circus.

DUMBO
2019

After the success of *Alice in Wonderland* in 2010, it made sense that Disney would want Tim Burton back for another of its live-action remakes of animated classics. At the time the studio invited him back, in the mid-2010s, these do-overs were the studio's primary cash cow. The three most recent, *Cinderella*, *The Jungle Book* and *Beauty and the Beast* had collectively grossed in excess of $2.5 billion and there were still plenty of films to choose from. For Burton's second go, they handed him *Dumbo*, the story of a little elephant with big ears and a bigger heart.

At first glance, it seems an odd fit. The 1941 animated version is almost entirely populated by animals – some talking, most silent – and cute critters are not really Burton's thing. The story centres on a baby circus elephant born with enormous ears, which initially makes him the target of bullying from the rest of the circus, including the elephants, and sees him separated from his beloved mother. When Dumbo reveals he can fly thanks to those ears, he becomes a star, whether he likes it or not. Eventually, he learns to believe in himself and finds his way back to his mother.

There are Burtonesque themes in there. Dumbo is unquestionably an outsider. He just wants to be himself and ultimately learns to ignore what others think. It's also set in a circus, a frequent Burton motif, and the 'Elephants On Parade' musical sequence from the original film is inventive and creepy in a way that isn't dissimilar to the songs in *The Nightmare Before Christmas*. There was something about it Burton connected to. 'I understood the idea of it, joining a weird family of outcasts who don't fit in with normal society – people who are treated differently', said Burton. 'That's what *Dumbo* is about.' You could see Dumbo as kind of a small, grey, wrinkly *Edward Scissorhands*.

BELOW: The film's spectacular look was created by Burton's long-time production designer Rick Heinrichs.

As was true of his *Alice in Wonderland*, Burton's *Dumbo* is actually vastly different from the original. Ehren Kruger wrote the script in 2014, well before Burton came on board. He eliminated all the talking animals – Dumbo's original sidekick, Timothy Q Mouse, is demoted to a squeaking cameo – and invented a story based around a fractured family. It's set in 1925, in a shabby circus run by Max Medici (Danny DeVito). One of his star acts, the marvellously named Holt Farrier (Colin Farrell), lost

ABOVE: Eva Green as trapeze artist Colette Marchant, a character invented for the film.

an arm in World War I and is unable to perform his old horse-riding act. Max gives Holt, plus his two children, Milly (Nico Parker) and Joe (Finley Hobbins), the job of looking after his elephants. When one of the elephants gives birth to the big-eared Dumbo, Max intends to dump this genetic oddity, until Dumbo accidentally flies during a clown show. Suddenly, Max wants to exploit Dumbo as his star attraction, but the Farriers just want him to live a happy life.

It isn't a bad expansion on the original. Holt echoes Dumbo's journey to embracing your difference as uniqueness, not disability, and Holt's children, who are separated from their mother by death as Dumbo is from his by force, mirror his coming-of-age narrative. It's a reasonably neat spin on the animated film. But that's only half the movie.

ABOVE: Michael Keaton as dastardly V A Vandevere, who wants Dumbo as the centrepiece for his amusement park.

Where the animated film ended, with Dumbo becoming a star on his own terms and freeing his mother, Burton's version takes off in a new direction. Dumbo's fame attracts the attention of V A Vandevere (Michael Keaton, working with Burton for the first time since *Batman Returns*) and his girlfriend, trapeze artist Colette Marchant (Eva Green). Vandevere owns a mega theme park and wants Dumbo at the centre of it. The extra 50 minutes – the original film ran for just 64 – don't really add anything deeper to the film's themes, but they do give audiences more spectacle for their buck. The 'Elephants On Parade' sequence from the original becomes a lyric-free bubble show, and while it isn't a match for the nightmarish phantasmagoria of the animated film, it's still beautiful. Unsurprisingly, unlike the 1941 film, that sequence doesn't begin with Dumbo accidentally getting drunk. Everything culminates in a CGI bonanza, Dumbo flying around the theme park, with Natalie on his back, to rescue his imprisoned mother.

The added pizzazz, though, isn't really to the story's benefit. One of the charms of the earlier film was its simplicity. Here, Dumbo gets rather lost in his own expanded world, a supporting character to the less interesting humans. Nobody could fault the effects team who brought this new Dumbo to life, with big expressive eyes to match his great flapping ears, but the film doesn't capture the heart in the same way that the original did – and still does.

Audiences reacted with a shrug. *Dumbo* is one of Burton's most expensive movies, with a jumbo budget of $170 million, on a par with *Alice in Wonderland*, but it made a very middling $340 million worldwide. Looking back on it later, some of its creators were less than enthusiastic. In 2024, while speaking to *The New York Times* about *Beetlejuice Beetlejuice,* Keaton said, 'I think I let [Tim] down on one movie. . .and it bugs me to this day. I was clueless on *Dumbo*. I sucked in *Dumbo'*. Rather hard on himself, perhaps, and most critics considered him one of the highlights, but Keaton's disappointment was nothing compared to Burton's. He went so far as to say he considered this film the end of his relationship with Disney, the studio where he had started his career, and which has been the home to some of his biggest hits and most defining movies.

'I started out [at Disney]', he said. 'I was hired and fired, like, several times throughout my career there. The thing about *Dumbo* is that's why I think my days with Disney are done. I realized that *I* was Dumbo, that I was working in this horrible big circus and I needed to escape. That movie is quite autobiographical at a certain level.'

Burton was so dissatisfied with the whole experience that he contemplated calling it quits on his entire career. 'I thought that could have been it, really', he said. 'I could have retired.' He didn't retire, thankfully. Instead, he took his career into entirely new territory.

Burton and The Killers

Burton has only ever made two music videos, both of them for the Las Vegas band The Killers. The first, *Bones*, is in part a tribute to the work of Ray Harryhausen. It begins with a couple watching the Harryhausen-directed skeleton fight from *Jason and the Argonauts*. As the video goes on, various characters, including the band, start stripping off their skin. A fun, if literal, interpretation of the lyrics.

The second video, *Here With Me*, is much more obviously Burton. A little like a twisted version of the 1980s comedy *Mannequin*, it has a young man becoming obsessed with a dummy of a woman (played by Winona Ryder). Black-and-white stripes and fairgrounds abound.

There was no grand plan to the collaboration. "We were just kicking around ideas for the *Bones* video, and we thought, Wouldn't it be great if Tim Burton could shoot this?", said the band's bassist, Mark Stoermer. "We reached out to his people and he came back and said he wanted to work with us." Which just goes to show that if you don't ask, you don't get.

'The juice is loose!'

BACK ON TOP

RIGHT: Wednesday Addams (Jenna Ortega) and her friend Thing (the hand of Victor Dorobantu).

WEDNESDAY
2022

It's almost laughable that it took close to 40 years for Tim Burton to work on an Addams Family project. There's probably no director working today who is more suited to America's favourite wholesome goths. Created by Charles Addams in the 1930s, the *Addams Family* cartoons depict a spooky (altogether ooky) brood who are unabashed killers and grave robbers, yet have no sense that they're anything other than a normal, happy clan. Parents

Gomez and Morticia, their two children, Pugsley and Wednesday, plus sundry other relatives, love each other dearly, but also like burying each other alive or torturing each other on medieval devices. There was never any particular narrative to the cartoons, but they're dark, funny and surprisingly sweet. Which is exactly what can be said of the best of Burton's work.

Burton loved the cartoons as a child, not just because of his affection for anything creatively sinister, but because they were easy to read. He didn't get on with comic books – 'I never knew which box to read' – and most *Addams Family* cartoons are conveniently just one panel. As he began to draw at school, he even realized his scratchy, exaggerated figures had a lot in common with Addams' work. He had not intended it, but the *Addams Family* had become part of his creative DNA.

Burton's name was mentioned in connection with various *Addams Family* projects over the years. Barry Sonnenfeld, director of the hit 1991 movie, said Burton was offered that film before him and turned it down, though Burton claims to have no recollection. There was a brief moment, in 2010, when he was rumoured to be prepping a stop-motion animated film about the family, but 'it never really went anywhere', he said.

As much as he liked them, Burton had never pursued an *Addams Family* project. He doesn't like to remake or 'reimagine' something if somebody else has already done it brilliantly. He learned that lesson on *Planet of the Apes*. There were already two great *Addams Family* films, by Sonnenfeld, and a terrific TV series from the 60s. He didn't want to do his version just to do it. But then he was offered an opportunity to approach the family from a new angle. It came along at probably the only time he would be open to doing it.

When the Covid-19 pandemic hit in 2020, the entire filmed entertainment industry shut down. By the time the United

ABOVE: Catherine Zeta Jones and Luis Guzmán, who first worked together on 2000's *Traffic*, play Morticia and Gomez.

Kingdom went into lockdown, in March of 2020, Burton had already been off work for months. After *Dumbo*, he wasn't sure what, if anything, he wanted to do next. 'I started isolating about a year before Covid', he joked. At that time, he received a script by Alfred Gough and Miles Millar, creators of the TV show *Smallville*. It wasn't for a film, but a TV show. If Burton wasn't sure if he wanted to direct another film, maybe he wanted to make something on the small screen?

Wednesday, as the title suggests, puts the spotlight on the Addams' only daughter. In Gough and Millar's imagining, Wednesday is packed off to Nevermore Academy, a boarding school for strange children, which is a complete nightmare for a child who hates other people's company and is demonstrably smarter than most adults. Not only does Wednesday have to reckon with – eurgh – teenagers, there's also someone committing horrible murders around the school grounds, and she seems to be the only person with the power to stop them. 'The one thing that terrifies Wednesday Addams is emotion', said Millar. 'What fascinated us as writers was exploring a character who starts out unable to have human connection and over the course of the first season moves that dial one notch.'

'I've felt like Wednesday since I was a teenager, even though I was a boy', said Burton. 'I wanted to see what she would look like in school, and how she would react to her family, and other people.' He had never harboured ambitions to work in TV, but this was an opportunity to dig into a character in a deeper way. Besides, it was the pandemic and he had plenty of time on his hands. Disillusioned with the film industry, this offered him a different way to flex his creative muscles. Initially, Burton thought he would direct all eight episodes of the series, until it was made clear to him that this would be a very hefty commitment, equivalent to making about three movies. Instead, he opted to direct the first four and produce the whole thing.

To play Wednesday, he hired Jenna Ortega, who had been a successful child actor on TV and was making moves into horror, with films like *X* and *Scream*, both 2022. Initially,

BELOW: Wednesday's (Jenna Ortega) little brother, Pugsley (Isaac Ordonez), feels the wrath of the school bullies.

Ortega was reluctant, because she had spent so long trying to break *out* of TV that she wasn't sure she wanted to go back in just as her film career was taking off. 'I got on the phone with Tim and. . .we kept talking and talking, and eventually I realized this is something that could be really interesting to be a part of', she said. As she had always been compared to Wednesday, thanks to her dry humour and serious resting face, she thought 'it just seemed fitting'.

Burton filled out the cast with Catherine Zeta-Jones and Luis Guzmán as Morticia and Gomez; Gwendoline Christie as the school principal, Larissa Weems; Emma Myers as Wednesday's far too perky school roommate, Enid; and in a sly casting coup, Christina Ricci as botany teacher Marilyn Thornhill. Ricci indelibly played Wednesday in the 90s movies. 'When [Christina] was on set, neither one of us said "Wednesday" once to each other', said Ortega of how she avoided imitating the role's defining actor.

You can see from the very first minutes that Burton is more creatively free than he has been in years. The show opens with a

BELOW: School principal, Larissa Weems (Gwendoline Christie) smiles through the horrors.

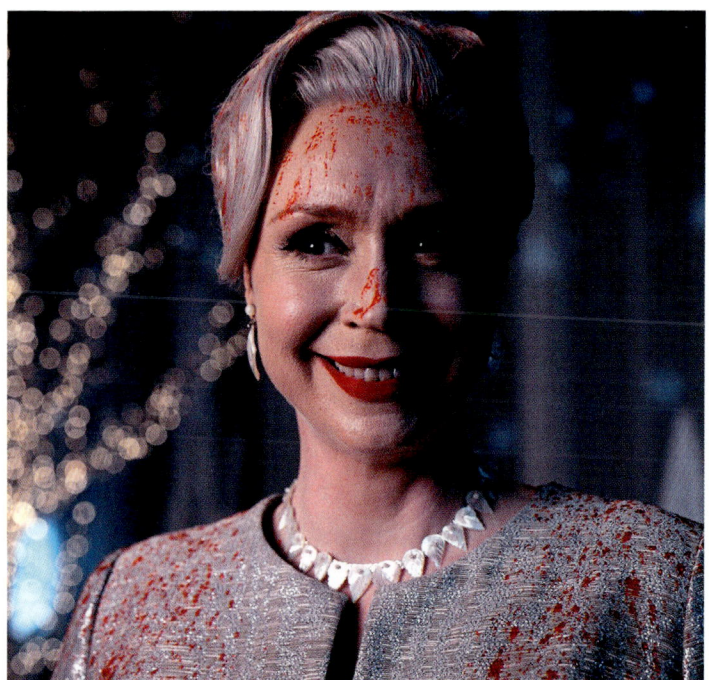

sequence at Wednesday's old school, Nancy Reagan High, with Wednesday taking revenge on the jocks bullying her younger brother, Pugsley (Isaac Ordonez). She heads to their water polo training session and releases piranhas into the pool. The editing of the sequence, equal parts horror and comedy, and the pay-off shot of a boy clawing his way up a ladder, then screaming into camera as the water around him turns a deep red, is vintage Burton.

As is often the case with TV shows in their first season, *Wednesday* is working out what it wants to be as it goes. Putting Wednesday in a school with vampires and werewolves, rather than ordinary children, sometimes feels like a missed opportunity for fish-out-of-water comedy, but for the most part it's a really good time. Ortega proves perfect casting, making Wednesday just human enough for audiences to invest in, while remaining true to Addams' deadpan creation. This Wednesday is allowed to smile, but only when something truly horrible happens.

The more leisurely running time of TV gives Burton the space to relax into his storytelling. His most recent films had been so convoluted in their plotting that he had lacked the opportunity for much of the incidental imaginative stuff that makes a Burton film truly Burton-y. *Wednesday* shows evidence of a director finding joy again. He has fun with references to his own past work and other horror classics. A bloody prom scene echoes Brian De Palma's *Carrie*, Weems seems to be cosplaying Kim Novac in *Vertigo*, and you might spot a taxidermy shop strewn with mice dressed as characters from Burton films, plus a tiny vermin Freddy Krueger.

Wednesday was a giant hit for Netflix, with the streamer reporting that the show had the second-highest first week viewership of any series on the platform, behind only *Stranger Things*. And evidently Burton was very satisfied with his little sojourn to the small screen, agreeing to return to direct another four episodes for the show's second season.

BEETLEJUICE BEETLEJUICE
2024

LEFT: Michael Keaton makes an eye-popping return to the role of ghost with the most.

Plenty of Tim Burton's films have spent a long time in development. *Edward Scissorhands* is based on an idea he had in his teens. *The Nightmare Before Christmas* took more than ten years to turn from a poem into a film. But none compares to the marathon gestation of 'Beetlejuice 2'. Fans had to wait 36 years between instalments.

It could have happened much sooner. There were plenty of attempts to get a second film going after the 1988 original became a hit, with lots of Burton collaborators taking a swing. Two scripts were commissioned in 1990. First Warren Skaaren, who worked on the first film, wrote *Beetlejuice in Love*, which would have taken the bio-exorcist to Paris, where he tries to steal the living fiancée of a man who plummeted to his death from the Eiffel Tower. That same year, Jonathan Gems, who would later go on to write *Mars Attacks!*, began work on *Beetlejuice Goes Hawaiian*. The sort of idea only a young Burton could conjure, it would have seen the Deetz family opening a hotel in Hawaii and building it on top of a sacred burial ground, angering an ancient spirit. You can guess who they have to call to try to smooth things over.

In 2015, Seth Grahame-Smith (*Dark Shadows*), got far enough along with a script that industry publications started reporting that a new film was on the cusp of getting a greenlight. However, after a 2017 rewrite by Mike Vukadinovich (*Rememory*; 2017), the project somehow faltered. Keaton said none of the scripts were worthy of a revisit to one of Burton's most fondly held movies. 'They just didn't get it', he said. Finally, a few years later, somebody did.

The core *Beetlejuice* quartet – Burton, Michael Keaton (Betelgeuse), Winona Ryder (Lydia) and Catherine O'Hara (Delia) – had been quietly talking about a reunion for years before it actually happened, but they swore each other to secrecy, because they didn't want to make anything public until there was a script they had full faith in. 'I didn't tell anyone. I didn't even tell my representatives', said Ryder, who recalls conversations began around 2012, when she and Burton were promoting *Frankenweenie*. It was only when Burton was working on *Wednesday* that Beetlejuice 2 gained momentum.

The original *Beetlejuice* was made in a very different era of Burton's career. As he had said before, it was one of the few times he had been left alone to do as he pleased. The latter part of his career had been spent under the studio microscope. As his films became more and more commercially successful, and therefore

The World of Tim Burton

With his unique style and propensity for sketching just about every idea he has, Tim Burton has become almost as well known for his art as his filmmaking. Exhibitions of his work have become hugely successful all over the globe. *The World of Tim Burton*, an installation of pieces from across his career, first opened in Prague in 2014. It has since travelled internationally in cities including Tokyo, London, São Paulo, Seoul and Mexico City.

more important to their distributors, countless execs and marketing partners had a view on how the film should play. He was at risk of his work becoming merely 'product'. The Tim Burton from the 1980s who had made films by just following instinct was almost a stranger, until Burton rediscovered that person in Romania.

In 2021, Burton was making *Wednesday* in Busteni, a little mountain town in central Romania. Directing a TV show isn't quite like directing a movie. Everything moves at great speed, because there are so many more scenes to get through. Burton found he loved it. It took him back to those early years, thinking on the fly; not stopping to second-guess himself, because there simply wasn't time nor money. 'It re-energized me a little bit', he said. 'It triggered things about *Beetlejuice* for me. And I thought, 'Well, none of us are getting any younger'. By this time he was just entering his 60s.

As he always does, Burton began sketching thoughts. He gave them to *Wednesday*'s writers, Alfred Gough and Miles Millar, and asked them to develop it into a screenplay. *Beetlejuice Beetlejuice* is a story about aging, evolving and accepting change. It finds Lydia (Winona Ryder) now in her 40s, the star of a tacky TV show in which she investigates ghostly goings on in people's houses. She's dating her smarmy producer, Rory (Justin Theroux), and is virtually estranged from her teenage daughter, Astrid (Jenna Ortega). When Lydia's father dies, she, Astrid and Lydia's stepmother, Delia (Catherine O'Hara), head back to their house in

BELOW: Delia Deetz (Catherine O'Hara) at the grave of her late husband, Charles.

ABOVE: Betelgeuse (Michael Keaton) is, yet again, trying to make Lydia (Winona Ryder) is awfully wedded wife.

Winter River to bury him. While there, Astrid gets involved with the wrong guy (Jeremy Frazier) and winds up trapped in the afterlife. And that unfortunately means Lydia is going to have to summon Betelgeuse in an effort to get her back.

There's also a subplot about Betelgeuse being hunted by his jilted wife, Delores (Monica Bellucci), and an investigation by a former TV cop turned afterlife actual cop (Willem Dafoe). And it all culminates in a wedding and lots of lip-syncing to 'MacArthur Park'.

If that all sounds disjointed and under-explained, that's because it is. The plot is peppered with holes and tramples logic, which is entirely in keeping with the first *Beetlejuice*. As *The New York Times* review said in 1988, 'There really isn't much plot here, only a parade of arbitrary visual tricks to hold the film together'.

Smooth narrative isn't the *Beetlejuice* vibe. Its attraction is in ingenious lunacy, of which this sequel has lots.

Michael Keaton had wavered on whether he wanted to return – 'there was a big, big, big, long period of time where I was like, don't touch it' – but he decided he would do it on two conditions: 'If I have any more screen time, it shouldn't be more than 30 seconds [more than last time]. . .and as little technology as possible. It needs to have that handmade feel.'

His instincts are absolutely correct. Betelgeuse is in the second film for about 17 minutes, a smidge more than last time. Every second counts. His scenes are easily the highlight of the film, with the same unpredictable, anarchic nature as the first. When he's not there, you miss him, but you also don't feel shortchanged. It's remarkable to think that Keaton was into his

BELOW: Lydia (Winona Ryder) and Rory (Justin Theroux) undergo some uninvited couples therapy.

70s when he made the film. His performance has just as much energy as he showed 36 years before.

As for the 'handmade' effects, that was no issue for Burton. He called the technology on the first film 'the worst effects of all time – but they're great'. *Beetlejuice Beetlejuice* has that same character, with a tangible quality to most of the special effects, rather than the all-too-frequent CGI chill. They don't always look real – when Astrid meets her dead father (Santiago Cabrara), who was eaten by piranhas, all the little fish attached to him are clearly animatronic – but they're not meant to look real. They're brimming with charm. They're at their peak in the final sequence, which has a stop-motion sandworm, Betelgeuse wearing fake bulbous eyes that look like a school craft project, and a frozen Willem Dafoe that's quite clearly a mannequin. And it's glorious.

Lydia's story, whether intentional or not, could be read as a mirror of Burton's over the past 40 years. A character who once marched entirely to the beat of her own drum, almost oblivious to how other people see her, has found herself making a successful, but phony, TV show. She's not sure when, or how, things went awry, but she has become a pastiche of herself. It's only by reconnecting with that old self that she finds happiness and fulfilment again. By the end, she has rediscovered who she truly is and couldn't give a damn what anyone else thinks.

Premiering the film at the Venice Film Festival in August 2024, Burton was in reflective mood. 'As you grow older, sometimes your life takes a bit of a turn', he said. 'I sort of lost myself a bit. . .This movie was. . .kind of getting back to the things I love doing, the way I love doing it and with people I love doing it with.' After a tumultuous decade and some stumbles so bad they almost made him want to end his career, Tim Burton had rekindled his love for movie-making and his confidence in himself. That little boy in the graveyard would be proud.

Resources

Chapter One

Feinberg, Scott, 'Tim Burton – *Wednesday* [LIVE]', Awards Chatter podcast, 2024

Freeman, Laura, 'Tim Burton: "I like monster movies, it doesn't mean I'm weird", *The Times*, 24 October 2024

Itzkoff, Dave, 'Tim Burton: At Home in His Own Head', *New York Times*, 19 September 2012

Kashner, Sam, 'The Class That Roared', *Vanity Fair*, 11 February 2014

'Late Night With Conan O'Brien', 18 November 1999

'Tim Burton Interview for *Vincent*', MTV [year unknown]

Pee-wee's Big Adventure

Edelstein, David, '*Beetlejuice*: Tim Burton, Michael Keaton on the Ghoulish Masterpiece', *Rolling Stone*, 2 June 1988

Feinberg, Scott, 'Tim Burton on His Life and Movies Coming Full Circle with *Frankenweenie*', *The Hollywood Reporter*, 18 February 2013

'Paul Reubens Panel', New York Comic Con, 2019

Salisbury, Mark, 'Burton On Burton', 2006

The Deadline Team, 'Oscars Q&A: Tim Burton', 17 February 2013

Thomas, Lou, 'Talking with Tim Burton', BFI, 15 September 2023

Trebay, Guy, 'Before There Was Pee-wee, There Was Pinky', 1 August 2023

Beetlejuice

Bassett, Lizzie and Winterbauer, Chris, '*Beetlejuice*', What Went Wrong podcast, 2 September 2024

Edelstein, David, '*Beetlejuice*: Tim Burton, Michael Keaton on the Ghoulish Masterpiece', *Rolling Stone*, 2 June 1988

Fallon, Jimmy, *The Tonight Show*, 20 August 2024

Lack, Hannah, 'There's Only One Winona Ryder', A*nOther Magazine*, 5 September 2024

McDowell, Michael and Wilson, Larry, 'Beetle Juice (2nd Draft)' script

Siegel, Alan, 'How *Beetlejuice* Was Born', *The Ringer*, 30 March 2018

'Tim Burton on making *Beetlejuice*', American Film Institute, 26 October 2020

Wilson, Larry, 'A Studio Executive Told Me the *Beetlejuice* Script Would Ruin my Career', *Film Courage*, 19 July 2017

Batman

Batman Production Notes, 1989

Breskin, David, 'Tim Burton', *Rolling Stone*, 9 July 1992

Feinberg, Scott, 'Tim Burton on His Life and Movies Coming Full Circle with *Frankenweenie*', *The Hollywood Reporter*, 18 February 2013

Gelb, Jeff, 'Sam Hamm', Comics Interview Super Special, 1989

Godfrey, Alex, '*Batman*: Michael Keaton on Justifying the Voice, Improvising Lines and More', *Empire*, 4 June 2023

Johnstone, Iain, 'Classic Feature: The Making of *Batman*', *Empire*, 8 May 2014

Morgenstern, Joe, 'Tim Burton, Batman and the Joker', *New York Times*, 9 April 1989

Ressner, Jeff, 'Three Go Mad in Gotham', *Empire*, August 1992

Tibbetts, John C, 'John C Tibbetts Interviews', 1989

Wan, Ben and Thunderwolf, Drew, 'Secrets of *Batman* 89', Superhero Stuff You Should Know, 3 October 2022

Edward Scissorhands

Breskin, David, 'Tim Burton', *Rolling Stone*, 9 July 1992

Elfman, Danny, 'Tim Burton', *Interview Magazine*, 11 January 2010

Fussman, Carl, 'Tim Burton: What I've Learned', *Esquire*, 17 December 2007

Itzkoff, Dave, 'Tim Burton: At Home in His Own Head', *New York Times*, 19 September 2012

Taylor, Trey, 'The Secret History of *Edward Scissorhands*', *Dazed*, 16 December 2015

Wente, Jesse, 'Tim Burton presents *Edward Scissorhands*', TIFF, 2010

Batman Returns

Breskin, David, 'Tim Burton', *Rolling Stone*, 9 July 1992

Burton, Byron, '*Batman Returns* at 25', *The Hollywood Reporter*, 19 June 2017

Couric, Katie, 'Tim Burton Interview', USA, 1992

De Vries, Hilary, 'Ready or Not : It's Back to Tim Burton's World', *Los Angeles Times*, 14 June 1992

Eller, Claudia, 'Burton's off *Reilly*', *Variety*, 4 May 1993

Godfrey, Alex, 'Burton Returns', *Empire*, July 2022

Goodfellow, Melanie, 'Tim Burton Talks Strange Phenomenon of Studio Career', *Deadline*, 21 October 2022

Hirshey, Gerri, 'The Bat's Meow', *Rolling Stone,* 3 September 1992

Ressner, Jeffrey, 'Three Go Mad in Gotham', *Empire*, August 1992

Woerner, Meredith, 'The Real Reason Marlon Wayans Passed on Playing Robin', *Gizmodo*, 4 August, 2009

The Nightmare Before Christmas

Aguilar, Carlos, '*The Nightmare Before Christmas*: A Hit That Initially Unnerved Disney', *New York Times*, 25 October 2023

Godfrey, Alex, 'Skellington Crew', *Empire*, January 2024

'The Making of *The Nightmare Before Christmas*' Walt Disney, 1993

'*The Nightmare Before Christmas* Turns 30: Danny Elfman on Creating Jack's Singing Voice', *Entertainment Tonight,* 2023

Yeend, Adam J, 'Henry Selick Reflects on 30 Years of *The Nightmare Before Christmas*', Academy of Motion Pictures Arts and Sciences, 11 October 2023

Ed Wood

Bergeson, Samantha, '*Ed Wood* Producer Denise Di Novi on Tim Burton's Classic', *Indiewire*, 9 August 2024

Bort, Matt, 'Johnny Depp talks about the movie: *Ed Wood*', Matt Bort, 1994

Gilchrist, Todd, 'Tim Burton on Why the *Batman* Films Have Changed and How *Beetlejuice Beetlejuice* Saved Him From Retirement After *Dumbo*', *Variety*, 22 August 2024

Maltin, Leonard; Maltin, Jessie, 'Tim Burton', Maltin on Movies, 30 September 2016

Milling, Robin, 'Johnny Handsome', *Cosmopolitan*, May 1995

Smith, Gavin, 'Tim Burton Interview', Film Comment, November–December, 1994

Vespe, Eric, 'Quint and the legendary Martin Landau discuss *Frankenweenie, Ed Wood*, bad actors and more!', *Ain't It Cool News*, 12 October 2012

Mars Attacks!

Adamek, Pauline, 'Tim Burton Interviewed for *Mars Attacks!*', *Arts Beat LA*, 1996

Feinberg, Scott, 'Tim Burton – *Wednesday* [LIVE]', Awards Chatter podcast, 2024

Jones, Ralph, 'The Oral History Of *Mars Attacks!*, Tim Burton's Misunderstood Sci-Fi Masterpiece', *Inverse*, 13 December 2001

Sleepy Hollow

Berry, Adam, 'Tim Burton's *Sleepy Hollow*': Giving life to an undying legend', ILM, 15 November 2024

DeCaro, Frank, '*Sleepy Hollow*: A Twitchy Take on a Tale of Terror', *New York Times*, 14 November 1999

Nashawaty, Chris, 'A Head of its Time', *Entertainment Weekly*, 19 November 1999

Rose, Charlie, 'Tim Burton on *Sleepy Hollow* and the fantastical vision of his films', Charlie Rose, 15 November 1999

Planet of the Apes

Horn, Steve, 'An Interview With Tim Roth', IGN, 20 June 2012

Horn, Steve, 'Interview with Mark Wahlberg', IGN, 31 July 2001

'Paul Giamatti Breaks Down His Most Iconic Characters', *GQ*, 20 Dec 2023

'Tim Burton on *Planet of the Apes*', *The Guardian*, 16 August 2001

Big Fish

August, John, 'Writing on Demand', johnaugust.com, 5 May 2009

Breznican, Anthony, 'Tim Burton: The not-so-grim reaper', *USA Today*, 8 January 2004

Gourley, Matt, '*Charlie and the Chocolate Factory* and *Big Fish* With John August', I Was There Too Podcast

Morgenstern, Joe, 'Tim Burton, Batman and the Joker', *New York Times*, 9 April 1989

Rose, Charlie, 'Tim Burton, Ewan McGregor, and Billy Crudup on the making of the film *Big Fish*', Charlie Rose, 9 December 2003

Russell, Jamie, 'Tim Burton – *Big Fish*', BBC, 24 September 2014

Charlie and the Chocolate Factory

August, John, 'Did I ever watch the original *Charlie and the Chocolate Factory*?' Johnaugust.com, 7 June 2004

August, John, 'How Long Should It Take To Write A Script?', johnaugust.com, 1 December 2008

'*Charlie and the Chocolate Factory*', BBC Norfolk, 29 July 2005

'Choc Talk', *Nickelodeon Magazine,* August 2005

Gourley, Matt, '*Charlie and the Chocolate Factory* and *Big Fish* With John August', I Was There Too Podcast

Horn, John, 'A Nuttier Chocolate', *Los Angeles Times*, 6 February 2005

Nashawaty, Chris, 'How Johnny Depp brought a new flavor to *Charlie*', *Entertainment Weekly*, 1 July 2005

Corpse Bride

August, John, '*Corpse Bride* article in *Script* magazine', johnaugust.com, 1 September 2005

August, John, '*Corpse Bride* has risen', johnaugust.com, 16 September 2005

Balfour, Brad, 'Tim Burton Marries the Dead', PopEntertainment.com, 25 September 2005

'Making Puppets Tick', Warner Bros EPK, 2005

Rowe, Robin, '*Bride* Stripped Bare', *Editors Guild Magazine*, July/August 2005

'The Making of *Frankenweenie*', Warner Bros, 2005

Sweeney Todd

Daly, Steve, 'Johnny Depp on cutting loose in *Sweeney Todd*', *Entertainment Weekly*, 3 November 2007

EW Staff, '*Sweeney Todd*', *Entertainment Weekly*, 11 December 2007

Gold, Sylviane, 'Demon Barber, Meat Pies and All, Sings on Screen', *New York Times,* 4 November 2007

Poland, David, 'DP/30: director Tim Burton', DP/30: The Oral History Of Hollywood, 4 January 2011

Pulver, Andrew, 'Tim Burton: 'When I first came to England I thought, "Wow! I'm home!"', *The Guardian*, 27 September 2016

Salisbury, Mark, 'Burton & Depp: Partners in Crime', *Los Angeles Times*, 2 January 2008

'The Making of *Sweeney Todd*', Warner Bros, 2007

Alice In Wonderland

Boucher, Geoff, '*Alice in Wonderland*' screenwriter is ready for haters: "It's audacious, what we've done"', *Los Angeles Times*, 8 February 2010

Raphael, Amy, 'Tim Burton: "Alice is a very annoying, odd little girl"', *The Guardian*, 6 March 2010

Rottenberg, Josh, 'Hollywood's Mad Hatter', *Entertainment Weekly*, 5 March 2010

Salisbury, Mark, 'Tim Burton and Johnny Depp interview for *Alice in Wonderland*', *The Telegraph*, 15 February, 2010

Weintraub, Steven, 'Johnny Depp and Tim Burton Interview *Alice in Wonderland*', *Collider*, 4 March 2010

Dark Shadows

Radish, Christina, 'Johnny Depp and Tim Burton Talk *Dark Shadows*', *Collider*, 8 May 2012

Richards, Olly, 'The Big Interview: Michelle Pfeiffer', *Empire*, June 2012

Taylor, Drew, 'Tim Burton Talks Making *Big Eyes*...', *Indiewire*, 18 December 2014

Frankenweenie

Adams, Tim, 'Tim Burton: 'The love and life and death stuff was stewing from the start', *The Guardian*, 7 October 2012

Breznican, Anthony, 'The strange true story of Tim Burton's normal hometown', 5 October 2012

Lammin, Daniel, 'Don Hahn, Disney Legend', *Switch*, 19 February 2013

Radish, Christina, 'Winona Ryder Talks

Frankenweenie, Reuniting with Tim Burton, and Why She Likes Dark Films and Characters', *Collider*, 5 October 2012

Richards, Olly, 'Little Horrors', *Empire*, September 2012

The Deadline Team, 'Oscars Q&A: Tim Burton', 17 February 2013

Young, John, 'Tim Burton talks about *Frankenweenie*', *Entertainment Weekly*, 12 May 2012

Big Eyes

'Amy Adams interview: 'My relationship with work feels healthy', *Time Out*, 23 December 2014

Breznican, Anthony, 'The strange true story of Tim Burton's normal hometown', 5 October 2012

Nakhnikia, Elise, 'Interview: Tim Burton Talks *Big Eyes*, Margaret Keane, and More', *Slant Magazine*, 20 December 2014

Taylor, Drew, 'Tim Burton Talks Making *Big Eyes*...', *Indiewire*, 18 December 2014

Miss Peregrine's Home For Peculiar Children

Eisenberg, Eric, 'The Hilarious Reason Tim Burton Had to Cameo In *Miss Peregrine*', *Cinemablend*, 30 September 2016

Freer, Ian, 'Professionally Peculiar', *Empire*, October 2016

Russo, Maria, 'A Book That Started With its Pictures', *New York Times*, 30 December 2013

Dumbo

Buchanan, Kyle, 'The *Beetlejuice Beetlejuice* Reunion Reunion: How It Came Together', *New York Times*, 27 August 2024

Dumbo Production Notes, 2019

Gilchrist, Todd, 'Tim Burton on Why the *Batman* Films Have Changed and How *Beetlejuice Beetlejuice* Saved Him From Retirement After *Dumbo*: "That Could Have Been It"' *Variety*, 22 August 2024

Goodfellow, Melanie, 'Tim Burton Addresses "Surreal" UK Politics; *Beetlejuice 2* & Why *Dumbo* Will Likely Be His Last Film With Disney – Lumière Festival Tim Burton Jamboree Continues', *Deadline*, 22 October 2022

Wednesday

Dilillo, John, 'Explore the Cavernous Halls of Nevermore with This *Wednesday* Easter Egg Guide', *Tudum*, 25 November 2022

Hailu, Selome, '*Wednesday* Debuts With Nielsen's Second Biggest Streaming Week of All Time', *Variety*, 21 December 2022

Lang, Brent, 'Barry Sonnenfeld on the 30th Anniversary of *The Addams Family*...', *Variety*, 14 October 2021

Ricci, Christina, 'Jenna Ortega and Christina Ricci Have a Cathartic Conversation About *Wednesday*', *Interview Magazine*, 20 October 2022

Richards, Olly, 'Her Dark Materials', *Empire*, November 2022

Vivarelli, Nick, 'Tim Burton Was Drawn to *Wednesday*'s Outsider Status for His First TV Series', *Variety*, 31 October 2022

Beetlejuice Beetlejuice

Buchanan, Kyle, 'The *Beetlejuice Beetlejuice* Reunion Reunion: How it Came Together', *New York Times*, 27 August 2024

Busch, Anita, '*Beetlejuice 2* Pushes Forward With New Writer at Warner Bros', *Deadline*, 12 October 2017

Godfrey, Alex, 'Back From the Dead', *Empire*, July 2024

Horowitz, Josh, 'Winona Ryder', *Happy Sad Confused*, 2 September 2024

Khomami, Nadia, 'Tim Burton admits he was a "little lost" in career before *Beetlejuice* sequel', *The Guardian*, 28 August 2024

Maltin, Leonard; Maltin, Jessie, 'Tim Burton', Maltin on Movies, 30 September 2016

Maslin, Janet, 'Ghosts and Extra Eyeballs', *New York Times*, 30 March 1988

Meyers, Seth, 'Michael Keaton on Reviving Beetlejuice', Late Night With Seth Meyers, 21 August 2024

Index

Bibliography

Burton, Tim; Walker, Andrew Kevin, *The Art of Sleepy Hollow*, Faber and Faber, 2000

Hughes, David, *Tales from Development Hell: The Greatest Movies Never Made?*, Titan, 2012

Jones, Karen R, *Mars Attacks: The Art of the Movie*, Titan, 1996

Salisbury, Mark, *Burton On Burton (Revised Edition)*, Faber and Faber, 2006

Woods, Paul A, *Tim Burton: A Child's Garden of Nightmares*, Plexus, 2007

Picture credits

Alamy Stock Photo: 4/5, 47, 120, 124, 127, 132, 134/135, 137, 140, 160/161, 163b, 172, 184/185: Movie-store Collection Ltd; 6: BFA/Warner Bros.; 8, 103, 145t, 149: ©Warner Bros./courtesy Max-imum Film; 10, 130/131, 143, 145b, 169: Warner Bros./Album; 13: TOHO/Album; 16, 60, 85: John Bingham; 19, 175: ©WALT DISNEY PICTURES/courtesy Cinematic Collection; 20: Steve Speller; 30/31, 37, 38, 40/41, 208, 212: ©Warner Bros./courtesy LANDMARK MEDIA; 32: GEFFEN FILM/WARNER BROTHERS/Album; 33: ©Geffen Pictures/courtesy LAND-MARK MEDIA; 34/35, 53, 98, 138/139: ©Warner Bros./courtesy PictureLux/The Hollywood Archive; 42: ©Warner Bros./courtesy AA Film Archvive/Allstar Picture Library Ltd; 44/45, 61, 72, 73, 78, 82/83: Pictorial Press Ltd; 48, 56, 65, 68, 81, 94, 100, 111, 128: Screen-Prod/Photononstop; 54: SNAP/Entertainment Pictures; 58, 63: ©20th Century Fox/courtesy Cinematic Collection; 66: ©Buena Vista Pictures/courtesy Everett Collec-tion; 71: kpa Publicity Stills/United Archives GmbH; 74, 77, 101: ©Warner Bros./courtesy Everett Collection; 84: ©WALT DISNEY/KELVIN JONES/courtesy Cinematic Collection; 86/87, 89: TOUCHSTONE PICTURES/Album; 91: ©TOUCHSTONE//courtesy AJ Pics; 92: ©Touchstone Pictures/courtesy LANDMARK MEDIA; 96: PAUL(PIBS)DAVIES; 104: ©PAR-AMOUNT PICTURES//courtesy AJ Pics; 109: MANDALAY PICTURES/Album; 110: Manda-lay/Constantin Film/IFA Film/United Archives GmbH; 112/113, 117: ©20th Century Fox/courtesy AJ Pics; 114, 118: ©20th Century Fox/courtesy Maximum Film; 122/123: ©COLUMBIA PICTURES/courtesy Cinematic Collection; 147, 151, 152, 164/165: ©WARN-ER BROS./courtesy AJ Pics; 154: ©WARNER BROS./courtesy Cinematic Collection; 156, 159: ©DISNEY/courtesy Maximum Film; 163t: ©DISNEY/courtesy AJ Pics; 167, 168: Pic-tureLux/The Hollywood Archive; 170: ©WALT DISNEY PICTURES/courtesy Album; 176, 194: TIM BURTON PRODUCTIONS/WALT DISNEY PICTURES/Album; 178, 180, 182/183: ©THE WEINSTEIN COMPANY/courtesy Cinematic Collection; 186: Photo 12; 188/189: © Twentieth Century Fox Film/Entertain-ment Pictures/ZUMAPRESS.com; 190/191: © Walt Disney Studios Motion Pictures/courtesy Everett Collection (Ron Harvey); 192/193: ©DISNEY/courtesy LANDMARK MEDIA; 195: ©DISNEY/courtesy Lifestyle pictures; 197: Tammie Arroyo/AFF; 198, 213: ©WARNER BROS./courtesy FlixPix; 200/201, 203, 206: Met-ro-Goldwyn-Mayer (MGM)/Album; 204/205: Vlad Cioplea/©Netflix/CourtesyEverett Col-lection; 211: dpa picture alliance/Alamy Live News; 214: ©WARNER BROS./courtesy Life-style pictures. **Getty Images:** 22, 25 Barry King/Sygma/Sygma; 29 Warner Bros./Handout.

Acknowledgements

Thanks, first, to all at Greenfinch and Quercus, especially Andrew Roff for asking me to write this book and Anna Southgate for making the editing process entirely painless. Big thanks to Dan Jolin for suggesting me for this instalment.

I'd never have met Burton if not for *Empire*, so thank you to all my editors past and present, particularly Colin Kennedy, Mark Dinning and Nick De Semlyen. And special mention to Alex Godfrey, as much of a Burton nerd as I am. I'm grateful for the sage advice of veteran authors Hayley Campbell, Eleanor Morgan, Helen O'Hara and Kat Brown, who patiently answered my many questions.

Finally, thanks to Max for keeping me company while writing and being a very good boy.